Y0-BUY-458

GROUP PROBLEM SOLVING
An Improved Managerial Approach

Harvey J. Brightman
Department
of
Decision Sciences
Georgia State University

HD
30.29
.B735
1988
West

1988

Arizona State Univ. West Campus Library

Business Publishing Division
College of Business Administration
Georgia State University
Atlanta, Georgia

Library of Congress Cataloging-in-Publication Data

Brightman, Harvey J.
Group problem solving :
an improved managerial approach / Harvey J. Brightman.
p. cm.
Includes index.
ISBN-0-88406-201-5
1. Problem solving, Group. 2. Decision-making, Group.
3. Organizational effectiveness. I. Title.
HD30.29.B735   1988
658.4'036—dc19   87-21876
                        CIP

Published by
Business Publishing Division
College of Business Administration
Georgia State University
University Plaza
Atlanta, Georgia 30303-3093
Telephone: 404/651-4253

©1988 by the College of Business Administration,
Georgia State University

All rights reserved, including the right to reproduce this
publication, or portions thereof, in any form without
prior permission from the publisher.

92 91 90 89 88   5 4 3 2 1

Georgia State University, a unit of the University System of
Georgia, is an equal educational opportunity institution
and an equal opportunity/affirmative action employer.

Printed in the United States of America.

Book design, cover design by Marcia L. Lampe

Phototypesetting by Donald E. Dedmon

To my mother and grandmother—of blessed memory

Edith Brightman   (1914–1965)
Sarah Brass   (1883–1978)

Thank you for putting up with all my problems.

CONTENTS

PREFACE

I completed my first book on problem solving in 1980. It focused almost exclusively on the individual problem solver. Even though I realized the importance of team problem solving, my research effort was still in its infancy. Now, eight years later, I would like to share with you what I have learned.

In his book, *Megatrends*, John Naisbitt argued that the ethics of participation has seeped into our values. People whose lives are affected by a decision must be part of the process of arriving at the decision. The shift to more participation came from the demands of the baby boomers coming of age and improving competition from abroad, especially Japan Inc. Naisbitt concluded that the new leader is a facilitator and team player, not an order giver. That is what my book is about.

Chapter 1 presents why and when you should consider a team problem-solving effort. I also provide an overview of my Constructive Conflict Model of team problem solving. Conflict within a team is useful as long as it remains professional, not destructive. Here I also distinguish between *disturbance* and *entrepreneurial* problems. The former are deviations from expected or historic performance levels (a sudden increase in absenteeism). Your job is to determine the causes of the disturbance. You face entrepreneurial problems as action requests from senior management (who should we assign overseas?) or when you seek new goals for your department or organization (how can we improve the productivity of our white-collar workers?).

Chapter 2 discusses why teams fail. We focus first on individual weaknesses—"judgment-making heuristics." We use these rules of thumb to help us make judgments quickly under ambiguity and uncertainty. Unfortunately they often produce poor decisions. Even stock market players succumb to these heuristics. In his book, *The Money Game*, Adam Smith said it this way, "We are a bunch of emotions, prejudices, and twiches and this is all very well as long as you are aware of them. If you don't know who you are, the stock market is an expensive place to find out. Wall Street or Main Street—it's all the same." Knowing our decision-making weaknesses is the first step toward improvement. The rest of the chapter concentrates on group-oriented problems. We examine how groups fail to communicate and how they mishandle conflict. When groups experience what sociologist Irving Janis calls groupthink, they make worse decisions than their weakest members do.

Chapter 3 describes general strategies for improving team success. First you will learn several methods to overcome ineffective heuristics. The approaches use all three problem-solving languages—verbal, visual, and mathematical. You then will learn seven general principles for leading effective team problem-solving meetings. Special attention is given to the Nominal Group Technique, a simple method for significantly improving team problem-solving performance. We conclude the chapter with a very detailed overview of my team problem-solving model.

The next three chapters form the core of the book. Chapter 4 focuses on team formation and problem finding. Carl Jung proposed that people collect information and arrive at judgments in systematically different ways—that we have different decision-making styles. You will learn why you should select team members with different decision-making styles. The chapter concludes with constructing a team charter and the art and science of problem finding. While problems eventually find us, effective managers are capable of sensing them long before they become crises. Chapter 5 presents the most critical phase of team problem solving—problem diagnosis and alternative generation. By using multiple cases, you will learn simple techniques to diagnose disturbance and entrepreneurial problems. You will also learn creative and logical methods for seeking and designing alternative solutions. In Chapter 6 you will learn rigorous, but nonmathematical, approaches for selecting a good option to solve your problem. You will also learn how to install your option when others do not play by the Marquis of Queensberry Rules.

Improving team success in practice is more than merely learning new problem-solving techniques. It requires departmental or organizational norms that foster creativity, trust, interteam cooperation, and learning. Unless these norms are firmly established, there will be little improvement. In Chapter 7 you will learn how to identify and change your departmental norms. When the proper norms are in place, you will then learn how to design programs that effectively train your staff in the new problem-solving techniques.

A book is never an individual effort. For three years as Research Professor I had the opportunity to pursue my research that led to this book. I want to thank publicly the College of Business Administration at Georgia State University. Also, I want to thank Cary Bynum, Peggy Stanley, and Claudia Forman of Georgia State University's Business Publishing Division for their help. Their careful editing and suggestions have improved the book. I hope you find it informative and readable. If so, why not tell others?

CHAPTER
O N E

INTRODUCTION

You are a member of a space crew originally scheduled to rendezvous with a mother ship on the lighted surface of the moon. Due to difficulties, however, your ship was forced to land some 200 miles from the rendezvous point. During the crash landing, much of the equipment aboard was damaged. Since survival depends on reaching the mother ship, you must choose the most critical items for the trip.

MAKING A CHOICE

The 15 items left intact and undamaged after landing are listed in Exhibit 1-1. Your task is to rank order the 15 items in terms of their importance in allowing your crew to reach the rendezvous point. Place the number 1 by the most important item, the number 2 by the second most important, and so on.

After you have rank ordered the items, ask members of your staff to form a team and also rank order the items. Do not be surprised if the team answer agrees more closely with NASA experts than your own. Under the proper conditions, groups can outperform single individuals. This book explains why. Incidentally, the answer to this problem can be found on page 224.

In this chapter we will answer the following questions:

EXHIBIT 1-1
The Moon Survival Problem

Box of matches	____	Life raft	____
Food concentrates	____	Magnetic compass	____
50 feet of nylon rope	____	5 gallons of water	____
Parachute silk	____	Signal flares	____
Portable heating unit	____	First aid kit including	
Two .45 calibre		injection needles	____
pistols	____	Solar powered FM	
1 case of dehydrated		transmitter	____
milk	____	200-pound tanks of	
Stellar maps (of moon's		oxygen	____
constellations)	____		

- Why should you consider forming managerial problem-solving teams?
- When should you form a team and when should you "go it alone"?

A group or a team is a collection of individuals who work and depend on one another. We know that people have formed a group when they work with one another, are interested in group rather than individual achievements, attend meetings, help colleagues, and refer to themselves as "we" and others as "they."

A group becomes a *problem-solving* team when it must solve a problem or make a decision. The group leader may reserve the right to make the final decision or permit and encourage the group to make the final decision. The former is an *information-sharing* team; the latter is a *participative problem-solving* team. Although they differ in the degree of power sharing, they are both problem-solving teams.

We often use groups because we believe that two plus two will equal five; that is, that team efforts are synergistic. Teams can be very effective. However, sometimes you will be more effective if you solve a problem or make a decision without any help from your subordinates or peers. What is important is that you should make an *explicit* decision as to whether or not to use teams.

Furthermore, groups are often so poorly run that their potential gains are not realized. Two plus two may equal one. The group may be worse than its best, or even its most typical, member. To overcome this you must select the right mix of team members. You also must manage the group's internal conflicts and ensure that they use the proper logical and creative problem-solving tools. How this can be done is captured by my *constructive conflict* model of team problem solving that is previewed in this chapter.

WHY MANAGERIAL TEAMS?

Managerial teams are an outgrowth of the emerging movement first identified by John Naisbitt.[1] American management originated the idea, exported it to Japan, and is only now "rediscovering" its power and potential. Three premises drive the participation movement:

• Under the right circumstances, managerial teams make better decisions.

• When workers participate in the decision-making process they "own" the decision and do not have to be sold on its merits.

• Increasingly, workers want to have a role in decisions that affect the quality of their working life.

Groups that are properly formed and managed can outperform their best members. Synergy is possible. Of course, this potential is not always achieved. But groups can draw on the resources of their members.

Often managerial teams are involved in installing a solution. The level of commitment of the installers is the key to success. If they have been involved in making the decision, they will work harder to make it work. The decision becomes their decision; they have a vested interest in making it work. Solution ownership is likely to occur when the installers have been members of the problem-solving team.

John Naisbitt has noted that participative decision making is on the increase. Earlier in this century, when American citizens stepped through plant or office doors, they were nearly rightless until 6:00 or 7:00 P.M. But over the years, this situation has been changing. These changes may be a result of the need to reconcile the contradiction between our democratic political values and archaic business traditions. Or perhaps American firms are taking another look at the value of worker participation, especially since Japan has been so successful in using worker-oriented quality circles. Remember that quality circles were an American idea. When they failed to take hold here, Japanese firms imported the idea and made it work. Only now are American firms realizing what they had and failed to use.

Regardless of the reasons, American firms are turning inward and attempting to involve workers in solving problems and making decisions. As Naisbitt stated, "the new leader is a facilitator, not an order giver." We are moving toward a collegial organization structure and away from the bureaucratic structure that predominated for many years.

The collegial structure rests on the following values and premises:
- Participation in the decision-making process
- Consensus generation
- Bottom-up flow of ideas
- Peer recognition
- Fighting hard for what you believe in but fighting in an above-board, fair, and clean fashion
- Information sharing
- Verbal communication[2]

Andrew Grove, chief executive officer (CEO) of Intel Corporation, believes that the collegial structure is particularly suited for rapidly growing scientific-based companies in the computer and telecommunications industries.[3] In the collegial organization, peer and networking relationships replace hierarchical relationships. Participation in decision making replaces autocratic decision making. The bottom-up flow of ideas complements the top-down flow of authority. Individuals are recognized for what they know, not for who they are. Information sharing replaces information denial and deliberate miscommunication. The collegial organization is especially necessary when the external environment changes rapidly, and the knowledge to understand and manage it does not reside within a single person. Managerial teams are an important mechanism for bringing about the collegial organization.

WHEN MANAGERIAL TEAMS?

This morning you found out that you have a series of important decisions to make over the next several months. The first decision you should make is whether to "go it alone," make the decisions after consulting with your subordinates individually, or make the decisions working within a problem-solving group. This is the *leadership approach decision*. Base it on three factors:
• Your effectiveness as a problem solver.
• Your subordinates and peers—their needs for involvement in decision making and the potential resources they bring to a team.
• The characteristics of the problem.

You, the Manager

Two issues are critical here: (1) Do you have sufficient information to make an effective decision? (2) How effective are you as a problem solver? Other things being equal, if you answer yes to both questions, make the decision alone.

Your Subordinates and Peers

Do your subordinates and peers have critical information? If you do not have access to this information, will you make a poor decision? If you answer yes to both questions, avoid "going it alone."

Do your subordinates and peers need to be involved in the decision process? Do you believe that they want or need to develop their critical thinking and creative skills? Do they need challenges, and is this problem such a challenge? Their need for involvement also depends on your demonstrated problem-solving skills as well as other demands on their time. If you are an excellent problem solver and they are swamped with other work, they may not wish to be involved in a problem-solving team effort. If you answer yes to these questions, avoid "going it alone."

Can you trust your subordinates and peers to deal with the problem without any hidden agendas? Are the organization's goals their goals? Is the ultimate solution likely to generate *excessive* or *destructive* conflict among your subordinates or peers? If you answer yes to these questions, you should make the decision after consulting your subordinates individually or you should organize a problem-solving team effort.

Finally, will your subordinates be involved in installing whatever solution you develop? If the installation will be difficult, then you should consider a problem-solving team effort.

Problem Characteristics

We can characterize problems along the four dimensions as shown in the following diagram:

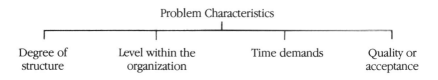

Problem Characteristics

| Degree of structure | Level within the organization | Time demands | Quality or acceptance |

Problems are well-structured when you have seen the problem before, when there is a consensus as to its causes, and when there is an agreed-on solution. Ill-structured problems are first-time-ever problems. They are wicked messes strewn with confusing symptoms, ambiguities, and uncertainties. You and your subordinates cannot agree on what the true problem is or how to solve it. For ill-structured problems, either consult individually with your subordinates or form a problem-solving team.

You can characterize problems according to the level at which they occur in the organization. Operational control problems require decisions to insure effective day-to-day operations. For example, how can we increase paperwork efficiency within the department? Or how can we reduce absenteeism? On the other hand, strategic planning problems involve setting policies, choosing long-term objectives, and selecting resources. Whatever action you take, it will be costly and will set precedent within the organization. The decision to build a second airport in Washington or IBM's decision to enter the microcomputer market are examples of strategic planning problems. The Tylenol scare at McNeilab Inc. produced strategic planning problems. An improper response could have bankrupted McNeilab. Use problem-solving teams when facing strategic planning problems.

Problems differ in the time available to solve them. Crisis problems demand immediate attention; they need to be solved today. Under these conditions, you alone should make the decision because there simply is not sufficient time to do anything else. But opportunity problems do not need to be solved yesterday; there is time to form a group to attack the problem. *These group problems are what we*

Also, there are quality problems and there are acceptance *will* problems. Solutions to acceptance problems are judged on *personal* *describe* *grounds*, either by yourself or by the group. That is, there is no *today* need to validate your judgment externally or present hard data in support of your position. The fact that you believe that a solution is best makes it best! The solution to quality problems must be judged on *external grounds*. You will have to prove to the project authorizers that your solution is an effective one. They will want to see hard data and an objective analysis. Because quality problems require more data, you should avoid "going it alone." In summary:

The Lone Eagle—Make the decision alone when:

- Time is limited.
- The problem is a well-structured operational control problem.
- You have all the needed information.

The Consultative Manager—Discuss with your subordinates before making the decision when:

- They have critical information.
- You will have to defend your decision to senior management.
- The problem is ill-structured.

The Team Manager—Form a problem-solving team when:

- Your subordinates have critical information and want or need to be involved in the final decision.
- You will have to defend your decision to senior management.
- You are facing an ill-structured strategic planning problem.
- Your subordinates will have to install whatever solution the team ultimately designs.

If you believe that your subordinates support the organizational goals behind the problem-solving effort, form a participative problem-solving team. Otherwise, form an information-sharing team.

CHOOSING A LEADERSHIP STYLE

Using the foregoing guidelines, which leadership style would you use in the following case?[4]

The Bank Location Problem. You are president of a small, but growing, bank with its headquarters in the state's capital and branches in several nearby towns. When you first bought the bank, it was in poor financial shape. You have significantly improved the bank's position, and your prestige in the banking community has increased. Your growth has been attributed to good luck and a few timely decisions. However, this has caused your staff to look to you for leadership. Although they are quite capable, you wish they were not quite so willing to accede to your judgment.

You have recently acquired the funds to open a new branch. Where should the branch be located? The choice will be made on simple common-sense criteria such as traffic counts, location of competitors, and future growth of the surrounding areas. Your managers are knowledgeable about the community and may be of great help in identifying suitable sites.

Their support is important as they will have to supply staff and technical assistance to the new branch to get it going. However, the success of the new branch will benefit all because it will strengthen the bank's financial position. You have always believed that the crucial key to success is senior management's esprit de corps.

Let's focus on you and your subordinates. You are an effective problem solver. Your recent track record proves this. However, your branch managers know the local real estate markets. They could be of great help in obtaining needed critical information. In the past your subordinates have shown a willingness to let you make the important decisions. And it seems they are not interested in getting involved in this problem. Nevertheless, you consider it important that they have the opportunity to grow as managers. Moreover, your branch managers must be committed to the decision because they will have to provide support services over and above their own branch needs. If you alone choose the site, their lack of enthusiasm may affect the quality of the support services they provide. You believe that they must own the decision.

Now consider the problem: There is no crisis to find a site. Rather, the site search is part of a long-term corporate growth strategy. However, the problem is an ill-structured strategic planning problem. You will use no magic formula to pick a site. Moreover, the bank has just recently begun to expand and has not had enough experience in site selection to develop an SOP (standard operating procedure). After the bank has made many site selection decisions, the problem will be well-structured. Moreover, you will have to defend the final decision with hard data to the bank's board of directors. Your personal assurances that a site is best will not be enough.

Which leadership style is appropriate? In this case, consider forming a problem-solving team to locate a site. Since your managers have not been involved in strategic planning problems before, form an *information sharing team.* You will reserve the right to make the final site selection yourself. But your managers will have had an opportunity to help you make a better decision. And they will grow as professional problem solvers during the process. Everybody wins.

A CONSTRUCTIVE CONFLICT MODEL OF TEAM PROBLEM SOLVING

Teams are particularly useful when solving ill-structured problems. The keys to solving fuzzy and wicked problems are to *create* and *resolve* doubt within the group. Doubt is the only guarantor of a good solution. For when group members prematurely agree on a course of action, they are often wrong. To create doubt, you need to foster *constructive conflict* within your team. Team members must learn how to generate differences of opinion and how to feel comfortable disagreeing with one another. Conflict is not bad as long as you keep it under control. When it is personal, it is destructive. But handled professionally, it will improve team performance.

The model shown in Exhibit 1-2 describes three major tasks in team problem solving. The interplay between critical, or convergent, thinking and creativity, or divergent, thinking within each task is essential. Creativity is exploratory, ideational, provocative, and possibility seeking. Critical thinking is goal-directed, logical, analytical, and seeks closure. Creativity creates doubt and critical thinking resolves it.

EXHIBIT 1-2
A Constructive Conflict Model of Team Problem Solving

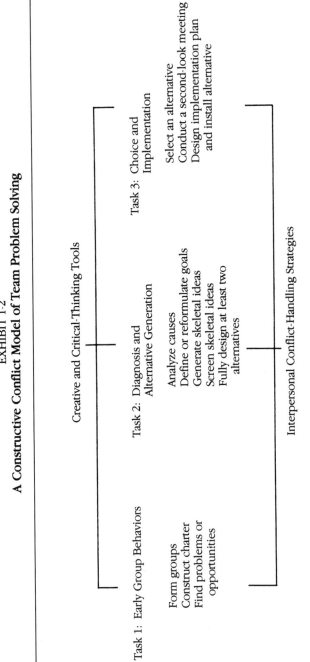

Creative and Critical-Thinking Tools

Task 1: Early Group Behaviors

Form groups
Construct charter
Find problems or
 opportunities

Task 2: Diagnosis and
 Alternative Generation

Analyze causes
Define or reformulate goals
Generate skeletal ideas
Screen skeletal ideas
Fully design at least two
 alternatives

Task 3: Choice and
 Implementation

Select an alternative
Conduct a second-look meeting
Design implementation plan
 and install alternative

Interpersonal Conflict-Handling Strategies

Early Group Behaviors

First you must decide who should be a team member. You have two strategies. You can select members who are either similar or dissimilar to one another. Similarity means people from the same department, with the same academic training, or who use the same methods to attack problems and make decisions. Team members who are similar will get along well with one another. They tend to form cohesive groups and there is little potential for conflict within the group.[5] Unfortunately, members who are similar may get along too well with one another. Similar members tend to think alike. It may be difficult to create doubt within a group. Instead of five views of a problem, you may have one view expressed five times. Therefore, even though dissimilar members will disagree, you should form heterogeneous groups.

Getting started correctly also requires that the group write a charter. The charter describes the group's understanding of the task, the constraints—time and budget—it will operate under, its formal place within the organization, and how it will operate as a group. For all but very temporary teams, writing a charter will improve group performance.[6]

Groups are often formed with a particular decision or problem in mind. For example, where should the new bank branch be located? Another type of group—what Gene Dalton, a management specialist, has called "venture groups"—has a mission to venture into the unknown.[7] A venture group's charter is to seek, adopt, and implement change within the organization. In short, its job is to innovate. The microcomputer development team at IBM is an example of a venture group. Within a mainframe-oriented company, the team's job was to design and launch the first-ever IBM microcomputer. It is fair to say that the group exceeded its own high expectations. Thus, for venture groups there is one additional activity within Task 1—the opportunity-seeking process. This entrepreneurial activity is often overlooked by teams or managers.

The first task of a group is to select its members, develop a charter, and then perhaps to seek out problems or opportunities. Charter construction is a logical process and problem or opportunity finding is a creative process. The tension between the two processes makes for effective early group behavior.

Diagnosis and Alternative Generation

This is the most critical phase in problem solving. Here you diagnose the problem and generate alternative solutions. What form problem diagnosis takes depends on the type of problem. A *disturbance* problem is a gap between your previous or budgeted level of performance and your present performance. When faced with a disturbance problem you must determine what factors caused the unexpected change in performance level. In short, you seek the causes of a problem and close the gap.

An *entrepreneurial* problem is a gap between your present performance and a higher or desired level. When faced with an entrepreneurial problem, you must determine how to reach higher levels of departmental performance. Here problem diagnosis means clearly defining the decision goals. Sometimes this is a straightforward process. We know the goals and we merely have to share them with others on the team. Sometimes, unless we reformulate the goals, we may not be able to solve the problem.

What exactly is goal reformulation? During the Peninsula campaign of the Civil War, General Meade asked President Lincoln for additional troops. He had 80,000 troops while the Confederates had 60,000 troops. According to the rules of warfare, in order to attack a fortified enemy, the attacking forces needed a 3:2 superiority. Given 60,000 Confederate troops, General Meade needed 90,000 troops—10,000 more than he had under his command. Now President Lincoln could have defined his goal as "how to obtain 10,000 more troops for Meade." He chose to reformulate. He told Meade to assume, for the moment, that his troops were on the defensive. But if the Confederates had 60,000 troops, all Meade needed to defend was 40,000 troops. The president told Meade that, with the now "additional" 40,000 troops, he should harass the enemy into a fatal mistake. Thus, rather than accepting Meade's decision goals, the president chose to reformulate. Reformulating goals can widen the search for effective alternatives.

Finally, we generate many "skeletal" ideas, screen them, and flesh out the best contenders into fully developed solutions. A skeletal idea can be written on a single page. It is an executive summary or overview. It should include a brief description of the idea, its rationale, and very rough estimates of the costs and benefits.

You then must reduce your list of ideas to a manageable size.

Your ultimate goal is to generate at least two *different* fully developed alternative solutions for formal evaluation. Generating only one alternative or two "clones" presents two problems. First, without a second legitimate contender, it is difficult to evaluate an alternative. When you can have any color car you want as long as it is black, you have no choice. Second, group members may be reluctant to review a single alternative thoroughly. For if the group ultimately rejects it, they will have to seek or create a second alternative and time may be limited. Thus, they may overlook some of the weaknesses of an alternative and magnify its strengths. Unfortunately, problem-solving teams often ignore this need for multiple alternatives and generate only one serious alternative for review.[8]

Unlike others, I do not separate the diagnosis and alternative generation processes—both are part of the second problem-solving task. The two processes must be interconnected. The alternatives you generate depend on your view of the causes. For example, suppose your new office automation system has not delivered the benefits you expected. If you believe that poor technology is the cause, you will seek additional technological alternatives. Alternatively, if you believe that your staff is deliberately sabotaging the system (cause), you will generate radically different alternatives. Diagnosis and alternative generation are two sides of the same coin. As you reconsider causes or new decision goals, you will naturally generate new alternatives.

The second task begins with either diagnosing disturbance problems or defining decision goals for entrepreneurial problems. After you have developed several "skeletal" ideas, you should screen them and then fully design at least two different solutions. Again, the interplay between creative and critical-thinking tools ensures success.

Choice and Implementation

The group now chooses an alternative, develops an implementation plan, and installs the solution. Too often authors recommend highly mathematical approaches for selecting the best alternative. Managers do not like and will not use these approaches. They are managers, not mathematicians. Yet we must develop rigorous methods that will help managers make the right choice.

You should then conduct a second-look meeting. Here you compare your chosen alternative against previously rejected options. Perhaps one of these options is better. The second look provides a final opportunity to identify the best option.

For all but trivial decisions, your team should develop an implementation plan. It should describe the steps and identify the personnel to successfully install the alternative. It covers who, what, when, where, and how.

Build your implementation plan on the following assumptions:
• The installation team will not be in place for the entire effort.
• Installation team members are not creative and possess exceptional judgment. Statistically speaking, too few people are exceptional. If they demonstrate these skills, you are ahead of the game.

When the solution produces major changes in the organization—for example, the initial introduction of office automation equipment—some individuals or groups will overtly or covertly oppose the change. These individuals may simply be uneasy about any change or they may believe that they will lose power or resources. We call these individuals or groups counter-implementors. They will do whatever is necessary to see that you fail. You must be ready to beat the counter-implementors at their own game. Conduct a potential problem analysis to determine where you might encounter implementation problems. Imagine that you have installed your solution. What can or will go wrong? What games will the counter-implementors play? What games can you play to beat them?

INTERPERSONAL CONFLICT HANDLING

Handling intergroup conflict is essential to problem-solving success. This is especially true for heterogeneous teams where the level of conflict is likely to be high. Consider the following five ways to handle conflict within your team (Exhibit 1-3):[9]

Competing is win-lose arguing. Members are assertive regarding their own positions but are unconcerned with other members' feelings or beliefs. Competers are dogmatic. They do not discuss, they argue. Conflicts are not resolved. Rather, reluctant team members are steamrollered into submission.

Avoiding occurs when a team member is neither assertive nor

EXHIBIT 1-3
Alternative Conflict Handling Approaches

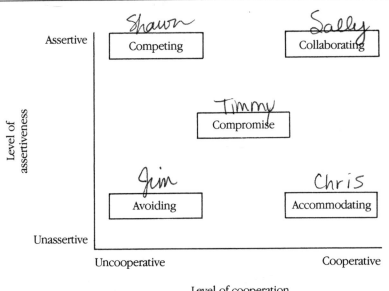

cooperative. The member fails to take a position and withdraws physically or psychologically from the group. Team members adopt a laissez-faire attitude that is best expressed as, "Why should we disagree? If you won't bother me, I won't bother you." Constructive conflict and effective problem solving are not possible under avoidance.

Accommodating occurs when a member is cooperative but not assertive in presenting a position. Group harmony is more important than effective problem solving. Here the goal is not to manage conflict, but to eliminate it. Often it works; however, the team pays a heavy price—ineffective solutions.

Compromise is seeking a middle ground between opposing positions. If you give, I will give, and we can reach agreement. Here you try to synthesize team members' ideas. The final solution contains the best of each person's thinking.

Most effective

✗ *Collaborating* is confronting disagreements openly to find solutions. It is fighting hard for what you believe in, but fighting cleanly. Here members *listen* to what others have to say. They attempt to find areas of agreement and to delineate carefully areas of disagreement. Members understand that through such a process the group will outperform its individual members. Disagreements must be professional, never personal.

While all of us have our favorite conflict-handling approaches, several researchers have suggested that the collaboration strategy is most effective.[10]

METADECISION MAKING

The goal of this book is for you and your team members to learn how to critique the processes you use in arriving at a decision. We call this *metadecision making*. Time should be set aside for your group to review how it operates. What are its strengths? What are its weaknesses? What can you do improve the problem-solving or interpersonal conflict-handling processes?

Even if groups are aware of what needs to be done to improve, will they do it? We know that it is difficult for groups to change the ways they operate. After all, people enter groups with a set of expectations as to how a group should operate.

This chapter has provided an overview of ways for managers to improve group problem solving. Throughout the remainder of the book I will discuss and provide examples of the techniques proposed here. My goal is for you to master and use these techniques. Improved group practices will not occur overnight, but with practice and patience, they will occur.

ENDNOTES

1. John Naisbitt, *Megatrends* (New York: Warner Books, 1982), 175.

2. Warren Bennis and Burt Nanus, *Leaders* (New York: Harper and Row, 1985), 122.

3. Andrew Grove, "How High-Output Managers Reach Agreement in a Know-How Business," *Management Review* (December 1983): 8–13.

4. Victor H. Vroom and Arthur G. Jago, "Decision Making as a Social Process: Normative and Descriptive Models of Leader Behavior," *Decision Sciences* (October 1974): 750.

5. Alvin Zander, *Making Groups Effective* (San Francisco: Jossey-Bass, 1982).

6. Irving Lane, et al., "Making the Goals of Acceptance and Quality Explicit," *Small Group Behavior* (November 1982): 542-54.

7. Gene Dalton, "Influence and Organizational Change," in *Organizational Behavior Models*, ed. Anant Negandhi and Joseph Schewitter, Comparative Administration Institute, Series No. 2 (Kent, Ohio: Kent State University, 1970).

8. Henry Mintzberg, Duru Raisinghani, and Andre Theoret, "The Structure of 'Unstructured' Decision Processes," *Administrative Science Quarterly* (June 1976): 246-75.

9. K. Thomas, "Conflict and Conflict Management," in *Handbook of Organizational Psychology*, ed. Marvin Dunnette (Chicago: Rand McNally, 1975).

10. Dean Tjosvold and Deborah Deemer, "Effects of Controversy Within a Cooperative or Competitive Context on Organizational Decision Making," *Journal of Applied Psychology* 65 (1980): 590-95; Marshall Poole, "Decision Development in Small Groups, III: A Multiple Sequence Model of Group Decision Development," *Communication Monographs* (December 1983): 321-41.

CHAPTER
T W O

WHY
TEAMS
FAIL

In the previous chapter we discussed why and when you should use managerial teams. Now we focus on why teams fail to live up to their potential. The organization's culture can stifle group effectiveness and creativity, team members may not be competent or creative, or the group may not operate as an effective team.

WHAT INEFFECTIVE TEAMS DO WRONG

Team members of ineffective groups exhibit some or all of the following seven characteristics:[1]
- Generate an incomplete definition of the problem and statement of objectives.
- Only seek or design one alternative solution.
- Do not reconsider alternatives rejected during the group's deliberations.
- Are poor information seekers and generators.
- Are ineffective problem solvers.
- Do not examine the risks associated with their chosen alternative solution.
- Fail to develop a contingency plan.

A team cannot solve a problem unless it is properly defined. Team members need to know its causes. Is it a marketing problem or is it an operations problem? Or are the causes traceable to both departments? In their rush to solve a problem, ineffective groups often ignore the critical diagnosis phase.

Meet Dr. X and Dr. Y. Both were excellent students in college and medical school. However, Dr. Y is an effective diagnostician, and Dr. X is not. Arthur Elstein and his associates wanted to know why.[2] Both doctors were asked to examine a patient with a most confusing set of symptoms. The 21-year-old was brought into the emergency room early one morning paralyzed in both her legs. The paralysis had occurred overnight. She is single, a college student, and has a casual boyfriend. She may be pregnant. The two doctors were not aware that the patient had already been diagnosed by the senior staff as suffering from multiple sclerosis (MS).

Dr. X's questions and medical workup were perfunctory since he was sure from the very start that the patient was suffering from conversion hysteria. He believed that the hysteria was caused by her possible pregnancy. He was wrong. Dr. Y also initially believed that hysteria was the most likely cause. However, he would not rule out other possibilities. He conducted an extensive medical workup and concluded she had multiple sclerosis. The lack of a diagnostic attitude is just as fatal to managers.

Ineffective groups often generate one or two solutions that are clones of one another and similar to present practice. For example, after the Vietcong attack on the U.S. airbase at Bien Hoa in 1964, the military considered three options:[3]

- *Option* 1. Continue to apply limited pressure on North Vietnam. Reject negotiations.
- *Option* 2. Gradually increase the level of military pressure. Publicly reject negotiations but privately recognize their inevitability.
- *Option* 3. Gradually increase the level of military pressure. Demonstrate a public willingness to negotiate.

The options are clones of one another. Radically different alternatives, such as developing a timetable for troop withdrawal or a direct attack on North Vietnam, either were never formally considered or were quickly rejected.

We call cloning the "muddling through" approach. Often it does not work, for if what we are presently doing has not solved the problem, making small changes is not likely to solve it either. Muddling through does, however, have one advantage. If the idea is effective, the team will have little opposition to installing it. Nevertheless, radically different ideas are often necessary to solve ill-structured problems.

Often, ineffective groups reject an idea with very little discussion. The idea's promoter may self-censor himself and believe that his idea is inferior to others on the table. Or the group may prematurely reject an idea. Once an idea has been rejected, it has little or no chance of ever being resurrected—"out of sight, out of mind."

Ineffective groups rely too heavily on an organization's information system, and fail to form ad hoc information-gathering teams. During a crisis problem, consider bypassing the normal communication channels for they may be too slow.

Of course, if team members lack the necessary critical-thinking skills, the group will be ineffective. We are not the critical thinkers we would like to be.

Ineffective groups frequently do not evaluate the risks associated with their alternatives. Furthermore, they fail to develop a contingency plan. The National Security Council under President Kennedy failed to consider the risks associated with the aborted Bay of Pigs invasion in 1962. A 1,400-man brigade was to land in Cuba and, with the help of a weak and highly ineffective "resistance" movement, overthrow the Castro regime. The National Security Council ignored numerous warnings that the plan was too ambitious. Moreover, the council never really considered that the attack would fail and, therefore, never developed a contingency plan. The rest is history.

That is not all. Ineffective groups have radically different communication patterns from those of effective groups (Exhibit 2-1).[4] Finally one researcher found that effective groups experienced short periods of conflict broken by prolonged periods of idea development; less successful groups had either too much or too little conflict.[5] This latter condition is called *groupthink*, and we shall have more to say about it shortly.

Until now we have described how ineffective teams operate. But why are they ineffective? In an earlier book I suggested three causes: (1) the culture of the organization, (2) the group's way of operating, and (3) the individual members.[6]

EXHIBIT 2-1
**Communication-based Differences
Between Effective and Ineffective Groups**

Members of Effective Groups:	*Members of Ineffective Groups:*
Examine the validity of opinions and assumptions.	Rarely challenge one another and treat opinions as facts.
Are more rigorous in evaluating solutions and compare solutions to the stated goals.	Evaluate solutions in a *perfunctory* manner.
Base their decisions on reasonable facts, inferences, and assumptions.	Rarely challenge questionable assumptions underlying their choices.
Have influential members who exert a positive facilitating influence; who ask questions, point out important information, or challenge the group to reject wrong arguments; who are *facilitators.*	Have influential members who exert a negative inhibiting influence; who stifle dissent, and are directive; who are *inhibitors.*

Organizations have their own ways of doing things. Behaviors that are acceptable at Apple Computer may not be acceptable at IBM. The corporate culture may improve or constrain your team's creativity and effectiveness. We know that:

- Organizations that operate in uncertain and dynamic environments are more likely to be creative.
- Organizations with young senior management are more likely to be creative.
- Organizations that nurture informality are likely to be creative.
- Decentralized organizations are more likely to be creative.
- Preoccupation with status and its associated symbols stifles creativity.
- Stressing the "one best way" of doing things stifles creativity.
- Never rewarding creative effort kills creativity.[7]

You can do little to change an organization's culture. However, a group's effectiveness also depends on its members and how they interact with one another. Shortly we will discuss these two controllable factors of group performance.

If you are presently leading a team effort, how effective is it?

Please take a few minutes to complete the questionnaire found in Exhibit 2-2. The questionnaire is taken from VanGundy, although the questions have been modified.[8]

Next we turn to examining the two causes of ineffective group performance—the team's members and how they interact with one another.

INDIVIDUAL FAILURES: PROBLEMS IN MAKING JUDGMENTS

Pogo once said, "we have met the enemy and we is they." A team's effectiveness is limited by the judgmental ability of its members. If they lack the intellectual ammunition, the team will misfire.

Judgments are plagued by inconsistency and systematic error. Good judgment requires a degree of mental skill and acumen that often exceeds our intuitive capabilities. We blame our poor judgments on other factors. As La Rochefoucauld noted, "Everybody complains about the badness of his memory, nobody complains about his judgment." Both experts and novices have trouble in making judgments, particularly when uncertainty or ambiguity is present. Yet it is for this very reason—the need to solve ill-structured problems—that we often form managerial problem-solving teams.

We have developed *heuristics* to help us make judgments under uncertainty. A heuristic is a rule of thumb that helps us arrive at a judgment about some event or make a decision. It serves to "simplify" judgment making.

We all use heuristics. For example, in the child's game of tic-tac-toe, you have learned that whoever goes first should place their X in the center square. This heuristic makes it difficult to lose the game. Or you have been asked to develop a food expense budget for next year. You could develop 365 daily meal plans and then cost them out. Or you could use the following heuristic. Take last year's food expenses and add 4% for inflation. Heuristics do simplify judgment making. However, they can also cause us to draw wrong inferences and improper conclusions.

Each of us has our own heuristics. However, researchers have

(*Text continued on page 27*)

EXHIBIT 2-2
A Team Effectiveness Questionnaire

Instructions: For each of the following statements, please circle the number that best describes your situation.

1 = strongly disagree   4 = agree
2 = disagree   5 = strongly agree
3 = neutral

THE ORGANIZATION CULTURE
The organization:

1. Encourages innovative ideas.	1	2	3	4	5
2. Believes in information sharing.	1	2	3	4	5
3. Provides resource support to install innovative ideas.	1	2	3	4	5
4. Encourages team problem solving and decision making.	1	2	3	4	5
5. Values cooperation and trust among colleagues (a "win/win" attitude).	1	2	3	4	5
6. Uses a bottom-up flow of ideas.	1	2	3	4	5
7. Stresses the importance of technical competence, interpersonal skills, or peer recognition rather than status differences.	1	2	3	4	5

Culture Score _____

GROUP FACTORS

Members of the group:

	1	2	3	4	5
1. Use collaboration or open confrontation in resolving conflicts.	1	2	3	4	5
2. Listen to one another.	1	2	3	4	5
3. Respect one another's beliefs and feelings.	1	2	3	4	5
4. Feel free to generate really different ideas.	1	2	3	4	5
5. Engage in professional conflict of ideas and positions.	1	2	3	4	5
6. Encourage everyone to participate.	1	2	3	4	5
7. Are task-oriented.	1	2	3	4	5

Group Factors Score _____

INDIVIDUAL FACTORS

Individuals in the group:

	1	2	3	4	5
1. Have a questioning attitude.	1	2	3	4	5
2. Are willing to assume risk and bear their ignorance.	1	2	3	4	5
3. Suspend judgment until all the data are in.	1	2	3	4	5
4. Are practical and seek data to support their positions.	1	2	3	4	5

Source: Adapted by permission of the publisher from *Managing Group Creativity*, Arthur VanGundy, pages 54–57, ©1984 AMACOM, a division of American Management Association, New York. All rights reserved.

(Continued)

5. Use logical or analytical tools to reach a conclusion.   1   2   3   4   5

6. Are possibility seeking/divergent thinkers.   1   2   3   4   5

7. Are disciplined or exhibit "stick-to-it-ness."   1   2   3   4   5

8. Are flexible in their approach to solving ill-structured problems.   1   2   3   4   5

Individual Factors Score _____

Interpretation: Add up the circled numbers and determine a total score for the three subcategories. Then compute the following Group Effectiveness Score.

$$(Culture\ Score/7) \times (Group\ Score/7) \times (Individual\ Score/8)$$

Average scores on the three subcategories can range from 1 to 5. Thus the Group Effectiveness Score score can range from a low of 1 (highly ineffective group) to a high of 125 (highly effective group). People enter and leave, teams change their ways, and there may even be changes in the organization's culture. You should evaluate your team or department every few months. If your team consistently scores under 60, this book is for you.

(Text continued from page 23)
also found heuristics that we all use. We will consider five such heuristics: (1) selective perception, (2) availability, (3) statistical regression to the mean, (4) representativeness, and (5) concreteness.

Selective Perception

Two researchers asked a group of 23 senior executives in a training program to analyze the problems facing the Castengo Steel Company.[9] Five of the 6 sales executives thought that the major problem was sales-related. Only 5 of the remaining 17 executives mentioned sales as a major cause. Four of the 5 operations executives thought that the major problem was related to production. Only 4 of the 18 other executives agreed. Only the vice presidents of public relations, industrial relations, and health services thought that the major problem was human relations-oriented. Here we have a prime case of selective perception.

Selective perception is the tendency to view problems from our own unique perspective. Our view of a problem is colored by our life experiences, education, and personality. What we see partially depends on who we are. We see with our mind as well as our eyes.

Sir Frederick Bartlett first studied selective perception over 70 years ago.[10] In one series of experiments he presented ghost stories from unfamiliar cultures to British college students. They read a story twice, put it aside, and reproduced it 15 minutes later. Thereafter, they generated reproductions at intervals of greater length, some as long as six years later. Bartlett found that there were common systematic distortions in the students' reproductions:

- *Leveling or flattening*—Most of the unusual details, unusual proper names, and unconventional writing style tended to fall out of the reproductions.
- *Sharpening*—A few details were retained and even exaggerated. The most accurate reproduction of detail occurred when it fit in with a student's prior interests and experiences. These familiar details became more prominent as the "leveling" occurred.
- *Rationalization*—The prose became more coherent and consistent with the reader's expectations and experiences. All references to ghosts and spirits in the folktales faded away and were replaced by familiar subject matter. The subjects were actively engaged in

"an effort after meaning"—an attempt to make sense of the original, but unfamiliar, story. Students also invented personal story elements to "fill in" the gaps in their version of the story.

Selective perception causes us to level, sharpen, and rationalize. We do not store a message detail by detail and then recall it on command. Rather, what is stored depends on our general impressions. And these depend on who we are. This is especially true when the meaning of the original prose is unclear or the problem is unfamiliar. Thus the sales vice presidents focused only on sales-related data in the Castengo Steel Company case. It was as if that data jumped out at them, while the remainder of the case was written in a foreign language.

Selective perception may even partially explain the debacle at Pearl Harbor.[11] Is it possible that General Walter C. Short, commander of the U.S. Army forces in Hawaii, misinterpreted the vague and ambiguous warnings of possible Japanese actions? And if so, might this be due to selective perception?

Short's major mission was to protect the naval fleet while in port. His second objective was to protect the Hawaiian Islands from an invasion. Throughout the year he had been warned of Japanese intentions to strike somewhere in the Pacific. On 27 November 1941, Short received the following urgent dispatch from General George C. Marshall, Chief of Staff of the U.S. Army:

> Negotiations with Japan appear to be terminated to all practical purposes with only the barest possibilities that the Japanese Government might come back and offer to continue. Japanese future action unpredictable but hostile action possible at any moment. If hostilities cannot, repeat cannot, be avoided the United States desires that Japan commit the first overt act. This policy should not, repeat not, be construed as restricting your course of action that might jeopardize your defense. Prior to hostile Japanese action you are directed to undertake such reconnaissance and other measures as you deem necessary but these measures should be carried out so as not, repeat not, to alarm the civil population nor disclose intent. Report measures taken. Should hostilities occur, you will carry out tasks assigned to Rainbow 5 (War Plan) so far as they pertain to Japan. Limit dissemination of this highly secret information to minimum essential officers.

General Short had three options:

Alert 1—Defense against sabotage and uprisings. No threat from without.

Alert 2—Security against attacks from hostile subsurface, surface, and aircraft, in addition to *Alert* 1.

Alert 3—Occupation of all field positions by all units, prepare for maximum defense of Oahu and the Army installations on outlying islands.

Short went on an *Alert* 1. He placed troops to guard the water, lights, gas, and oil facilities on the island. He huddled his unarmed aircraft at the air bases to protect them from sabotage. He stored the antiaircraft ammunition in locked and guarded magazines. He operated the radar Air Warning System (AWS) and Information Center for an additional three hours a day—from 4:00 A.M. to 7:00 A.M. However, the center was understaffed to respond to an actual air strike on Oahu.

Short did *not* (1) undertake reconnaissance; (2) inform the Navy that he had been ordered to undertake reconnaissance (long-range reconnaissance was the Navy's responsibility); or (3) offer planes to the Navy to begin reconnaissance. He continued to maintain his aircraft on four-hour notice. Given the maximum range of the radar, his planes could not scramble and intercept an attacking force even if they were detected. He continued to maintain his training schedule for ferrying pilots and aircraft to the Philippines. For the most part, it was business as usual.

In 1946, a Joint Congressional Committee reviewed Short's decision to go on *Alert* 1 status.[12] They rejected his reasoning. Army commanders in the Panama Canal, West Coast, and the Philippines had all undertaken reconnaissance after they had received the same "war warning" message. Moreover, General Short should have conferred with Admiral Husband E. Kimmel concerning the need for reconnaissance. Finally, they concluded that General Short should have stopped training and undertaken reconnaissance to protect the fleet in port.

How can we explain General Short's decision to go to an *Alert* 1 status? He was a competent and hard-working officer. Perhaps selective perception colored his thinking and caused him to abstract the wrong meaning from the war-warning dispatch. Here are some key phrases from the dispatch and the actions General Short undertook:

Dispatch	Action Taken
". . . but hostile action possible at any moment."	Went on *Alert* 1 (threat from within). Also ordered AWS (radar) to operate additional hours from 0400 to 0700 daily.
". . . you are directed to undertake such reconnaissance and other measures as you deem necessary."	No reconnaissance undertaken. Also, Short did not ask the Navy to undertake reconnaissance.

To comprehend General Short's actions, we must understand the man. His thinking was colored by three factors:

1. A widely-held assumption about the Japanese.
2. His extensive experience in combat and training.
3. His lack of experience in, and understanding of, the Army Air Corps.

Like many Americans, Short believed that Japan could not launch a successful air attack on the fleet at Pearl Harbor. In February 1941, Congressman Charles Faddis of Pennsylvania had declared, "They (Japan) will not dare to get into a position where they must face the American navy in open battle. Their Navy is not strong enough and the homeland is too vulnerable."[13]

General Short believed that any air attack would be a prelude to an all-out assault on Oahu.[14] An attack would be accompanied by sabotage and most likely would occur when the fleet was *absent* from port. As a field commander, General Short was preoccupied with the German model of warfare—the worming from within, followed by an aerial blitzkrieg, ground battle, and occupation. Even though his major mission was protecting the fleet in harbor, protecting the islands from invasion was always on his mind. Short was so preoccupied with the German model that *after* the air attack on Pearl Harbor he went on *Alert* 3 status. He was clearly awaiting an all-out invasion of Oahu. He could not believe that Japan's mission was to "merely" sink the naval fleet.

It appears that General Short's eight years of experience in military training also colored his thinking. Although not his main mission, training became his passion. Colonel George W. Bicknell, Short's assistant for intelligence, said, "he got so wrapped up in the training business that he could not see the other issues at stake." Training had now become more important than the protection of the fleet. Colonel Walter Phillips, General Short's chief of staff, agreed with the decision to go to an *Alert* 1. Not surprisingly, Colonel Phillips also had extensive training experience. In fact, General Short testified that one reason he liked Phillips was because of the training experience he brought to the post.

This was Short's first command of an Army Air Corps unit. His lack of experience caused him to undervalue its worth. Perhaps this was one reason he trained enlisted air corps personnel in antisabotage and combat tactics during the spring of 1941. Now training for combat was something that Short could understand. Furthermore, he testified in 1946 that even if he had been on an *Alert* 3, the low-flying Japanese airplanes would still have been able to do their damage. Four years after the attack on Pearl Harbor, Short still did not recognize the potential of fighter aircraft to neutralize a hostile air strike.

Let us speculate how General Short could have misinterpreted General Marshall's war-warning dispatch. When he read "hostile action is possible at any moment," perhaps he reasoned as follows:

1. Hostilities will not begin in Oahu for several reasons: (1) the fleet is still in port and therefore Japan won't dare attack the *islands*; (2) the nearest Japanese troops are several thousand miles away; therefore, there is no need to go to an *Alert* 3.
2. But hostilities will occur in the Far East, probably in the Philippines. Therefore, my most important job is to continue and accelerate the training. Thus I must increase the *training* hours for the AWS/radar system.
3. Although an attack is unlikely here now, the Japanese will begin the first phase of the German model. Given a large percentage of Hawaiians of Japanese descent, they will initiate sabotage. If we can stop them, we may be able to force Japan to rethink its future invasion plans. Therefore, I must institute an *Alert* 1.

We are all susceptible to selective perception, and sometimes we pay a heavy price.

Availability

Please answer the following questions before reading on.

1. Is the letter "k" more likely to be the first or third letter in an English word?

2. Are the letters "re" more likely to be the first two or last two letters in an English word?

If you think that "k" and "re" are more likely to be at the beginning of a word, you are not alone. That is how most people respond. When asked why, they usually say that they can remember more words that start with "k" than have "k" as their third letter. These people have used the availability heuristic and are wrong. The letter "k" is two times as likely to be the third letter. The *availability heuristic* occurs when managers' judgments of an event's probability are based (or biased) by the number of instances of that event that they remember and the ease with which they come to mind.

The *availability* of instances is affected by such factors as recency and salience that are unrelated to the correct probability. Let us see how availability works. You are asked to estimate the number of highway deaths due to DUI (driving under the influence). If you had recently read a story of a young child being killed by a drunk driver, you are more likely to overestimate the actual number. Given the saliency and recency of the story, you would probably generalize this one instance and overestimate its probability.

Paul Slovic, a noted decision theorist, demonstrated that even experts are subject to the availability heuristic.[15] He asked experts to estimate the number of deaths per thousand due to a variety of diseases and natural causes. Here is what he found:

Most Overestimated	*Most Underestimated*
1. Motor vehicle accidents	1. Smallpox
2. Abortion	2. Diabetes
3. Tornado and floods	3. Stroke
4. Botulism	4. Tuberculosis
5. Cancer	5. Asthma
6. Homicide	6. Emphysema

Deaths that make the headlines are overestimated; quiet killers are underestimated. Clearly the probability of an event is not affected by the ease with which we can recall instances from memory. For as you now know, selective perception influences what we remember. There may be no relationship between stored memories and the correct probability.

Statistical Regression to the Mean

In 1981, a professional baseball player called BB batted .297. The next year he batted .207. Many baseball experts agreed that BB had "lost it" after a brilliant year (have you noticed that the word "brilliant" is overused in sports). Was his career over? Was it all downhill from here? After all, he had batted 90 points higher in the previous year. Or is there an alternative explanation to his poor year?

Many of us fail to understand the concept of random variation. For example, all steel-belted tires from one manufacturer will not have the same tread life. Some might last only 25,000 miles, others might last 60,000 miles. The tread life varies because the conditions under which the tires are made varies. The manufacturing plant uses multiple batches of raw material, and no two batches are identical. The plant produces tires on different machines at different times of the day by different workers. These thousand-and-one differences account for the variation in tire life. We know this and are not surprised.

Likewise, human performance may vary from day to day or year to year. While we recognize this variation concept when we talk about inanimate objects such as tires, we often overlook it when it comes to people and their performances. Maybe random variation can explain BB's alternating excellent and mediocre performances.

Up until 1980, BB was, on the average, a .240 hitter. When he batted .297 he and others *logically* assumed that he had developed his skills and was about to become a star. There is, however, another explanation. His .297 year was far above his average level of performance. Thus if he was not really improving, we would expect that he would drop below his average level of performance in the following year. That is, bad years tend to follow good years. And that is what he did. Thus his "poor" performance can be explained as simply as his "outstanding" performance. Both are *random variations* around his long-run average performance.

It is possible that his .297 year signalled the transition from journeyman ballplayer to star. If that were true, he would have continued to have excellent seasons over the next several years. He did not. What the experts failed to recognize was the concept of *statistical regression to the mean* (SRM): When performance increases over long-run average levels and the individual or team has really not improved, we would expect that performance would subsequently degrade or regress toward the long-run average.

Perhaps our experts would have thought of SRM if they had plotted BB's batting average over the last several years (Exhibit 2-3).

EXHIBIT 2-3
BB's Batting Averages

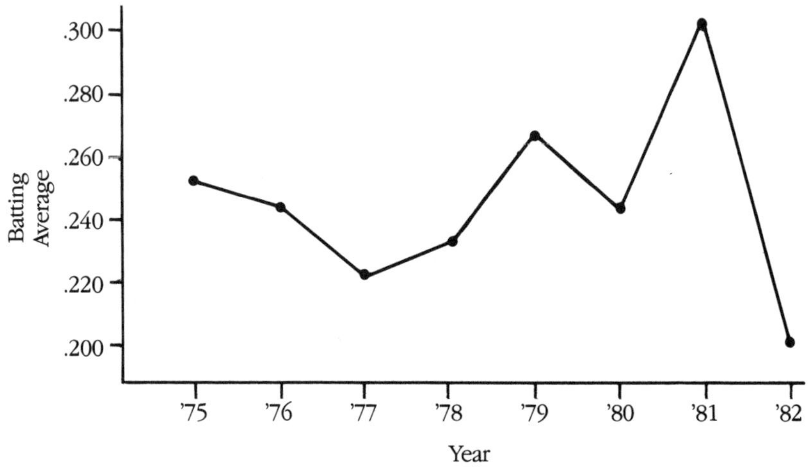

From 1975 to 1980 BB's average fluctuated around .240. Some years were higher and some were lower. But there was no systematic upward trend in his performance. The variation from year to year appears to be random. The laws of probability tell us that a mediocre year is likely to follow an outstanding year, unless BB's long-run performance level is about to increase.

The lesson is clear. When an individual or group suddenly shows a significant improvement in performance, you must consider two explanations:

1. There has been a real increase in performance that should be followed by subsequent high levels of performance into the future.
2. There has been *no* increase in performance. What you see is merely random variation, and, in the future, the level of performance will regress to the long-run average.

Unfortunately, managers (baseball and business) often forget the second explanation and it may be costly. Several years ago at a pilot training program, the senior officer believed that by using positive reinforcement he could improve his trainees' performance levels. He publicly praised those pilots who flew an effective mission. To his dismay he found that, instead of continuing to improve, the praised pilots did worse on their next mission. This seemed to violate the concept of psychological conditioning. What he failed to understand is that unless pilots really do improve, if they do well one day they will tend to do poorly the next day whether they are praised, reprimanded, or ignored. Consider the concept of SRM in evaluating the performance of individuals or teams over time. Remember, there is "no variation like random variation."

Representativeness

The following is a brief description of a high-school senior written by a school psychologist:

> Harvey is intelligent. However, he lacks true creativity. He has a need for order and clarity, and is very detail-oriented. His writing is rather dull and mechanical, occasionally enlivened by flashes of imagination of the science fiction type. He has a strong drive for competence. He seems to have little feeling and sympathy for other people, and does not enjoy socializing or working with others. He has a deep moral sense of right and wrong.

Harvey is currently considering graduate school.

1. If you believe you have enough information, please rank order the top four fields of graduate study that Harvey is likely to major in. Assign a rank of one to the most probable choice, a rank of two to the second most probable choice, etc.:

Business administration	____	Physical sciences	____
Engineering	____	Law	____
Computer sciences	____	Social work	____
Humanities	____	Library sciences	____
Education	____		

2. If you do not believe you have enough information to rank order the fields, what *specific* information would you need?

Did you rank order the fields based on the similarity between Harvey's personality and the demands of the field? For example, Harvey has little feeling or sympathy for others. Thus, it is unlikely that he will major in social work for he probably does not have the right people skills. Clearly the match between Harvey's personality and the job requirements—what we call *representativeness* data—is an important piece of information.

However, we cannot yet make a valid judgment about Harvey's graduate major. We need one additional piece of information— the percentage of all graduate students majoring in the nine fields. This is *base rate* data. Managers use the representativeness heuristic when they ignore base rate data in making probabilistic judgments. Rather, they focus their predictions on what appears most representative of the evidence. Statistical reasoning mandates that both representativeness and base rate data be used.

It is appropriate to compare Harvey's profile with the demands of the various graduate disciplines. Certain fields attract certain personalities. A shy and retiring person may not be an effective used-car salesman. However, it is wrong to focus solely on representativeness data. You must factor in the known base rate data. This is your anchor point.

Suppose that 40% of all graduate students major in business administration. Without even knowing Harvey, we would assign a 40% chance that he will major in business. Now we factor in Harvey's personality and adjust upward or downward our initial base rate estimate. We might increase the 40% figure because his profile is typical of an accountant or financial analyst. Here is a diagram of the adjustment approach:

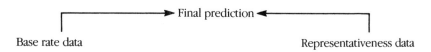

Base rate data   Representativeness data

Do we have both the representativeness and base rate data in the following two probabilistic judgment problems?

The Seismic Test Problem. Before a well is drilled, oil companies frequently conduct seismic tests to determine if there is oil. They drill a hole in the ground, insert a dynamite charge, and detonate it. The test indicates either that oil is likely or unlikely. The test is not perfect.

Of those wells where we found oil, 70% of the seismic tests had indicated that oil was likely. Of those wells where we had not found oil, 75% had indicated that oil was unlikely.

Can you estimate the chances of finding oil if the seismic test says that oil is likely? If so, make an educated guess and circle one of the figures below:

0%   10%   20%   30%   40%   50%   60%   70%   80%   90%   100%

You might be tempted to say that the chances of striking oil if the seismic test says oil is likely is 70%. But you cannot because all you have is representativeness data. These are the 70% and 75% figures in the second paragraph of the problem statement. For example, of those wells that struck oil, the seismic test had indicated that oil was likely in 70% of them. However, we do not have *base rate* data; that is, the chances of striking oil in this field. Without base rate data, you cannot use the simple model just shown. If you knew the base rate probability, you could then adjust it upward or downward based on the representativeness data. Exhibit 2-4 displays a comparison of base rate and representativeness data for the graduate student and oil field problems.

EXHIBIT 2-4
Base Rate and Representativeness Data

	Graduate Student	*Oil Field*
Goal	Chance of Harvey majoring in various subjects given his personality.	Chance of finding oil given that seismic test says that oil is likely.
Base rate data	Without knowing Harvey, the percentage of majors in the various disciplines.*	Without knowing results of the seismic test, the chances of finding oil.*
Representativeness data	Match between Harvey's personality and the demands of the various majors.	Match between how often oil was found when seismic tests said that oil was likely.

* These probabilities were not given in the problems.

The Computer Scanning Problem. A computer company uses a scanning device that places a mark on each defective chip it spots in the production line. The quality control department reports that 20% of all chips are defective.

When a chip is okay, the scanner correctly leaves it unmarked 90% of the time. When the chip is defective, the scanner marks it as defective 90% of the time. Do you have sufficient data to *estimate* the chances that a computer chip is really defective if the scanner marks it as defective? If so, make an educated guess and circle one of these figures:

0%   10%   20%   30%   40%   50%   60%   70%   80%   90%   100%

In the second paragraph you are given the representativeness data. For example, when a chip is defective the scanner marks it as defective 90% of the time. You are also given the base rate data in the first paragraph; that is, 20% of all chips produced are defective. You then start with the 20% figure and should adjust it upward. If any chip on the line has a 20% chance of being defective, would you not agree that one marked as defective has a higher chance of being defective? Especially since of all the defective chips, 90% are marked as defective. Compare the three problems of this section in Exhibit 2-5.

In the next chapter I will present a simple visual aid to determine the exact probability when you have both the base rate and representativeness data.

Concreteness

Several years ago I decided to purchase a used automobile. As you may know, *Consumer Reports* conducts surveys to determine which cars have the fewest repair problems. Based on the survey, I had decided to purchase one of their recommendations. Several days before actually purchasing the car, I was discussing my choice with a colleague. He told me that he had that model car and that it was the worst lemon in the world. In one instant I changed my mind. I had just succumbed to the concreteness heuristic.

The *concreteness heuristic* occurs when an individual places greater weight on highly personal data over abstract or impersonal data. What affects decision making is the source of the data, not its sample size. This flies in the face of statistical reasoning.

Let us review my decision-making process. The survey, based on several thousand people, reported that the model needed very

EXHIBIT 2-5
Base Rate and Representativeness Data

	Graduate Student	Oil Field	Computer Chip
Goal	Chance of Harvey majoring in various subjects given his personality.	Chance of finding oil given that seismic test says that oil is likely.	Chance of finding a defective chip given it is marked as defective.
Base rate data	Without knowing Harvey, the percentage of majors in the various disciplines.*	Without knowing the results of the seismic test, the chances of finding oil.*	Without knowing the results of the scanner, the chances of the chip being defective.
Representativeness data	Match between Harvey's personality and the demands of the various majors.	Match between how often oil was found when seismic test said that oil was likely.	Match between how often a defective chip is marked as defective.

* These probabilities were not given in the problems.

few repairs. On the other hand, a close friend told me that his car was a real lemon. I valued his information (based on a sample of one) much more heavily than the *Consumer Reports* data (based on a sample of several thousand). I did not know the survey people, but I knew my friend. His personal and concrete experiences caused me to change my mind—the concreteness heuristic in action.

Unless the survey data are questionable—improper sample size or biased wording of the questions—large-size samples are more meaningful than a sample size of one. Placing greater weight on a sample size of one violates statistical reasoning.

The concreteness heuristic occurs also in the business world. The senior management team of a pharmaceutical firm is discussing how to respond to the precipitous drop of their best-selling product. The patents had recently expired, and their competitors who sold generic equivalents were eating into the company's sales and profits. The company was considering raising the price of the drug in hopes of convincing doctors and pharmacists that it was a high-quality product. The company had recently conducted a scientific market research study that showed that raising the price would not convince anyone. Yet the company chose to raise the price. During the deliberations, one of the senior people strongly argued that he *personally* believed that the higher-price strategy would work. Without much discussion, the group bought his idea and rejected the marketing research results. The group members had succumbed to the concreteness heuristic and later they paid the price. the price.

Highly personal data should not be given greater weight than abstract data. What is important is the validity of each and the amount of evidence that supports each position. Other things being equal, large-size samples should be more convincing than small-size samples.

In this section we have discussed some of the heuristics that managers misuse in making judgments or reaching decisions. Pogo was correct—we *are* our own worst enemy. Teams cannot be effective when their members succumb to these and other ineffective heuristics. Simply knowing that heuristics exist and can plague our thinking is the first step in overcoming them.

TEAM FAILURES: GROUP DYNAMICS PROBLEMS

Even if all team members were wise, the group may not operate effectively. Poor group operations can overwhelm highly competent team members and cause the group to perform worse than its best or even average member. We call these operations "group dynamics."

The noted psychologist, Kurt Lewin, coined this term during the 1930s and 1940s. The movement took off after World War II and became a major focus in the field of psychology. During the 1950s and 1960s group dynamics was popularized and sometimes misunderstood. Malcolm Bradbury, a British writer, offered this amusing, if somewhat cynical, definition:

> You know how you feel uncomfortable at parties when you haven't fastened your flies. Well, that's Group Dynamics. . . . Group Dynamics is based on the discovery that the reason why people disagree with one another is that they are different and they have perceived a simple solution which will abolish all conflict: you simply make all people the same.[16]

Recently there has been renewed interest in group dynamics. Unlike earlier periods, researchers are now interested in making groups more effective rather than developing theories. Whatever the focus, group dynamics is about the nature of the psychological and social forces working within groups. It focuses on the nature of groups, how they develop, and their effect on individual members, other groups, and larger institutions. In this section we will focus on four highly interrelated factors that can negatively impact group dynamics and, ultimately, decision-making effectiveness: (1) communication, (2) conflict handling, (3) group size, and (4) cohesiveness.

Communication

The communication process contains four elements:[17]

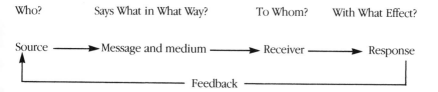

| Who? | Says What in What Way? | To Whom? | With What Effect? |

Who and To Whom. Status refers to a person's rank within a firm, and is legitimized by the trappings of one's office—status symbols. J. Forester, an observer of the "Status Race," noted that the sheer volume of office real estate and its quality are important status symbols in Great Britain.[18] In British government, a permanent secretary is allowed up to 550 square feet, a deputy secretary up to 450 square feet, and an under-secretary up to 350 square feet, and so on down to a typist who gets 60 square feet. Higher-status managers get larger desks made of finer grades of wood. Senior people get 8-foot desks, and junior managers get 5-footers. Directors get wall-to-wall carpeting, and managers have carpet squares. Hardly the collegial organization.

Status affects who speaks to whom within a group. From a variety of studies, the following pattern emerges:

• Higher-status members talk more frequently to one another.
• Lower-status members talk more frequently to higher-status members than to other lower-status members.

What is more, the amount of interaction is related to one's status or rank within group. As shown in Exhibit 2-6, high-status members monopolize the conversation.

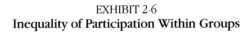

EXHIBIT 2-6
Inequality of Participation Within Groups

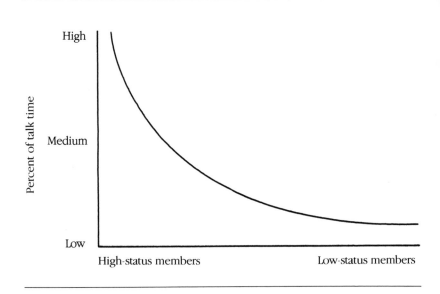

If we record the amount of time (not the quality of what is said) that members at different status levels speak within a group, we find a common pattern—an exponential curve. High-status members speak significantly more than do lower-status members. The percentage of talk time drops very quickly with status. Thus, low-status people hardly speak at all. They may defer to authority, not want to disagree with their superiors, or believe that what they have to say is not important. For whatever reason, they choose not to speak.

Unless the group leader or the group structure motivates them to participate, low-status members may sit back and observe the meeting. This places a heavy responsibility on the high-status members. Since they monopolize the conversation, they better know what they are talking about. In the collegial organization, this status-oriented communication pattern is unacceptable. All group members must participate. If equal participation is an unrealistic goal, then we should strive to flatten out the curve.

Women, irrespective of their formal position, are often treated as low-status members. Yes, Virginia, sex discrimination does occur in group meetings. The unequal level of participation is exacerbated when women are a numerical minority. In a study of workers' councils in Yugoslavia, females in male-dominated groups spoke less than their male counterparts and made fewer attempts at running the meeting.[19] One reason was cultural. The women believed that they were "outsiders" in a male-dominated world. In fact, male members asked females only questions of fact and did not ask them to share their beliefs and opinions.

Without proper group leadership or structure, male group members will often dominate the group's discussion (even when the group is chaired by a female), refuse to be influenced by female members, and expect females to defer to their beliefs and opinions.[20] In short, females are often treated as second-class team citizens.

The Message. Both the spoken and written word can be garbled. Perhaps the written language is more ambiguous for there are no effective ways to convey the rich nuances of spoken language—tonal stress, pauses, and gestures. Paul Watzlawick, a psychiatrist, offers some interesting examples of garbled messages.[21] What do you think they mean?

1. Air Force bars sending parcels to Vietnam.

2. Topless club loses appeal.

3. Customers who think that our waiters are rude should see the manager.

Are officers' clubs on Air Force bases sending parcels to Vietnam or is the Air Force prohibiting parcel shipments to Vietnam? When the message is ambiguous, we simply do not know. We become confused, search for concrete and understandable information, and attach great meaning to it.

When a message is ambiguous, its meaning depends on who is reading it. Unfortunately, many people naively assume that there is only one correct (read here, their own) explanation.

Even in face-to-face interaction, speech is a complicated process. Language not only conveys information but also expresses a worldview. To an optimist, a problem is only a minor irritation that can be cleared up quickly. To a pessimist, the same problem is a disaster. Our definition depends on who we are. There is room for distortion, uncertainty, and, ultimately, conflict.

Nonverbal communication has its own set of problems. Every gesture, posture, or facial expression conveys its own meaning. Nonverbal behavior can reinforce speech or contradict it. When a manager continually shifts around in the chair and fidgits with a paper clip, but says there is time to talk about your problem, what is the real message? We will improve our communication skills when our body and mouth speak with one voice.

The Effects. When two people speak, how does the receiver understand what the sender is saying? The process is called *encoding,* and it is open to error. There is no guarantee that "what was sent was heard and understood." Robert Krauss, a psychologist, paired off four-year-old children and separated them by a screen.[22] Each child was given a set of blocks with different designs. One child (the encoder) was told to describe the designs to the other child (the decoder). After several successful attempts, the encoder was given the number "three" to describe to the other child. He kept referring to it as *sheet.* Of course, the decoder could not guess the design. When Krauss asked the encoding child why he called the number "three" a sheet, he responded: "Have you ever noticed that when you wake up in the morning, the bed sheet is all wrinkled? Well, sometimes it looks like this."

In order to transmit the proper meaning, the encoder and decoder must be on the same wavelength. They must speak the same language. If not, there will be "noise," not meaning. We do not hear with our ears, we hear with our minds. And we are different from one another. All of us suffer from selective perception. What we hear depends on who we are. Remember, words are not the events themselves; they are a translation of the events into language. No translation is perfect. *Beware the translator.*

Conflict Handling

Here we are concerned with two issues: (1) the level of conflict and (2) how it is handled. Ineffective groups experience prolonged periods of conflict punctuated by short periods of problem solving.

These cycles of frustration repeat over and over again until the group is physically or mentally exhausted. Alternatively, ineffective groups may not experience enough conflict. Everyone is happy and content. But the group may fail.

The level of conflict depends, in part, on the group's cohesiveness. Cohesiveness refers to the extent to which group members are attracted to one another and to the group. In highly cohesive groups there is more communication, greater cooperation, and less conflict. But groups can be too cohesive, and experience too little conflict. Ultimately this can result in *groupthink*.

Ineffective groups do not know how to manage the conflict within the group. Conflict is not always bad. Whereas effective groups manage conflict through collaboration or compromise, ineffective groups use competition or avoidance. Competition forces members to choose sides in a dispute; there are winners and losers. Members are assertive regarding their own positions but are unconcerned with other members' feelings or beliefs. Avoidance is the failure to take a position. Members withdraw physically or psychologically from the group. While the potential for conflict is minimized, so is the potential for creativity. Avoidance has a high price tag.

Group Size

The optimal size of a group is between five and seven members. For optimal *communication*, teams should not have more than seven members.[23] For optimal *problem solving*, teams do best when they have about five members. In a study of how teams of managers and MBA students solved the NASA Moon Survival exercise presented at the beginning of this book, researchers found that performance increased as group size increased from three to five members. Group performance declined thereafter.[24]

Often it is necessary to form larger groups. Solution installers or others who have a vested interest in the decision are invited to join the team. As part of the problem-solving team, installers are likely to work harder and smarter in implementing the solution. Stakeholders, representing those constituencies who are affected by the decision, must also be team members. Often a "good" decision fails because the team forgets to invite interested, and often opposing, parties to join. It is better to know your opponents and face them directly than to ignore them. Affected stakeholders also provide different perspectives of a problem that may be critical in solving an ill-structured problem.

Stakeholders get involved in decisions that are important to them. The question is when—while the decision is being made, or after it has been made? Afterward they may resort to "stonewalling" and other strategies to smother a solution. This, of course, may happen even if they are invited into the group. But you cannot reason with a faction that is not represented in the group. If you believe that communication is a road to understanding, you will invite important stakeholders to join your team.

Given the need for installer and stakeholder involvement, groups are likely to exceed five members. As the group size increases, communication becomes more difficult. The size of the group greatly affects how often a member can talk and how much he or she expects others to talk. The larger the group, the smaller the proportion of people who can have the floor. When groups have more than eight members, consider dividing the team into several subgroups. Each member then has the opportunity to speak within a subgroup. Once the subgroups have reached a position, call a plenary session. Now each subgroup can present its ideas to the others and attempt to reach a consensus.

Add team members with care. Communications and cohesiveness are reduced with increasing group size. My rule of thumb is,

- *Teams* should have less than eight members.
- If that is not possible, effective *subgroups* should have six or fewer members.

Group Cohesiveness

Cohesiveness depends on the strength of members' desires to remain members. Cohesiveness increases as members become attracted to the group, view the group as "we," and take a more active role in the group's work. With increasing cohesiveness, group members speak more often, listen more carefully to others, influence one another more often, and adhere more closely to group norms or standards. Greater cohesiveness can also produce more pressure for unanimity of position and less tolerance for deviation from the group's ideology and thinking. Members will not hesitate to sanction deviant members and bring them back on line. Finally, by sharing or withholding group rewards, a cohesive group gains additional influence over its members.

The firm's culture and reward structures also affect the level of team cohesiveness. In a collegial organization we would expect managerial teams to exhibit high levels of cohesion. In internally competitive organizations we would expect less team cohesion. For better or worse, a managerial team often reflects the culture of the total organization. In Japan, business firms bind their employees to the company by recruiting friends from the same school and assigning them to work teams. This corporate practice also helps to create cohesive managerial teams.[25]

Reward systems tell us about the organization's intent to build cohesive teams as well. Bonuses and salaries based on team performance will produce cohesive teams if the team members are attracted to one another. If bonuses are based on individual performance, then team cohesion may suffer.

Cohesiveness is necessary for group functioning. Can you imagine how ineffective a team would be if the members found the task uninteresting and did not like one another? There would be anarchy. However, groups may be too cohesive and may exhibit groupthink.

GROUPTHINK

The sociologist Irving Janis argues that highly cohesive and long-lived groups are susceptible to groupthink. Groupthink is a consensus-at-any-cost mentality and produces a serious deterioration in a team's problem-solving capabilities. Members suppress their personal beliefs and criticism of others' ideas to allow the group to reach agreement with minimal conflict. While the group leaders may not cause the suppression, they may do nothing to stop it. A group adopts an informal rule or *norm* that can be expressed as, "For the sake of the group's harmony and the need to take action, I will withhold any personal doubts." We call this the "norm of mutual reciprocity," and it often leads to poor decision making (Exhibit 2-7).[26]

EXHIBIT 2-7
Janis's Model of Groupthink

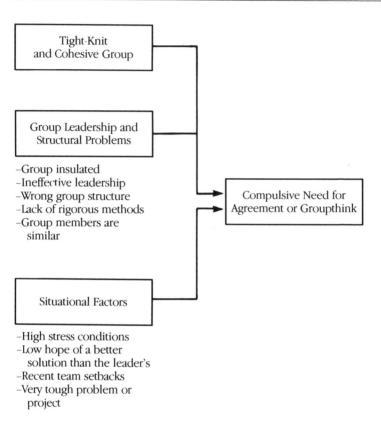

Source: Reprinted with permission from *Groupthink: Psychological Studies of Policy Decisions and Fiascoes,* by Irving Janis (Boston: Houghton Mifflin, 1982), 244. Modified with permission of The Free Press, a division of Macmillan, Inc. from *Decision Making: A Psychological Analysis of Conflict, Choice, and Commitment* by Irving L. Janis and Leon Mann. Copyright 1977 by The Free Press.

Groupthink has a number of antecedent conditions.[27] Beyond cohesiveness, ineffective group practices and stress-producing situational factors are necessary for groupthink.

Group Insulation
Groups that are physically or psychologically insulated from others can be less effective. Fresh perspectives are needed to challenge

the members' current, and perhaps unrealistic, thinking and ideas. Someone must say that the emperor is not wearing any clothes. When groups are insulated, their members look to each other for support and may lose touch with reality.

Ineffective Leadership

The group leader may not possess these critical leadership skills:

* *Listening and Clarifying Skills*
    1. Avoid interrupting others.
    2. Pay attention to feelings.
    3. Summarize ideas and feelings frequently.
    4. Do not be overly critical of your group members.
* *Supporting and Encouraging Skills*
    1. Encourage all to speak.
    2. Avoid promoting your own solution early in the group's discussion.
    3. Do not manipulate others.
    4. Help group members to build on each other's ideas.
* *Creating Constructive Conflict*
    1. Encourage and protect minority opinion.
    2. Assign members to critically evaluate solutions.
    3. Deal with disagreement openly.
    4. Seek out multiple solutions to a problem.

Wrong Group Structure

Often the group leader is unaware that there are alternative ways to run and lead the team. The most common approach is the discussion group structure. A discussion group really has no structure. Group members speak when they have something to say; otherwise they remain quiet. Discussion groups can be effective but there are more effective ways to run and lead a team.[28]

Lack of Rigorous Methods

Frequently group members accept claims made by other members without challenging them. Claims are treated as gospel. Previously we discussed how a senior management team reacted to a major drop in sales of their most profitable drug. In discussing the "raise the price and promote the quality" option, a senior executive said, "I'm sure that if we raise the price, doctors will still prescribe our drug. They are price insensitive; all they care about is their patients."

No one in the room challenged that statement. After the meeting, the executive was asked how he knew that doctors would react positively to a price raise. He said, "Last night I had supper with my brother-in-law who is a doctor. He told me that his patients' well-being was his only concern—cost was no barrier." I wonder how many of the executives would have been willing to buy that claim if they knew it was based on one doctor's beliefs. Why we accept what others say at face value is a great mystery of the universe. But when it happens, problem-solving effectiveness suffers. Managers need simple, yet powerful, critical-thinking tools. Stay tuned.

Group Member Similarity

Group members should not be clones of one another. If they are, there is a risk of having one member represented in five different bodies, not five different members. Group members who are alike can be myopic in their analysis of a problem. For example, to a group of engineers a problem is always an engineering problem; to a group of psychologists it is something quite different. For example, an owner has received a number of complaints about the slowness of elevators in his high-rise building. An engineering team would probably suggest the following: (1) install faster elevators or (2) install express elevators; that is, have one bank of elevators service the first 20 floors and a second bank service floors 21 to 40. Seems quite reasonable if you are an engineer. We expect engineers to develop *technological* solutions. After all, they are engineers. A team of psychologists might suggest the following solutions: (1) install mirrors on each floor or (2) place coffee and doughnuts on each floor. Both options give tenants something to do while they wait for the elevators. Psychologists develop *human-oriented* solutions. A team of psychologists and engineers could be very effective if they could work with one another.

It is not always possible to have a variety of different disciplines within a group. After all, departments often recruit from a limited number of college majors. Thus departmental teams will often be composed of members with similar backgrounds. But even within a discipline not all people are alike. We collect and process information differently from one another. That is, we have different *decision-making* styles.[29]

Situational Factors

Groupthink is more likely to occur when group members are under severe stress, when the team has had some recent setbacks, or when everyone thinks that the leader's solution cannot be improved. Everyone is looking for a way to end the agony. And they find it by reaching premature consensus.

Symptoms of Groupthink

When teams reach premature consensus, you are likely to see team members:

1. Discount warnings about what others (the enemy or competitors) may do.
2. Fail to examine critical and underlying assumptions.
3. Stereotype others.
4. Place heavy pressure on dissenters.
5. Self-censor themselves.
6. Have a shared illusion of unanimity.
7. Stop the flow of information that is contrary to the group's position through self-appointed mindguards.

When groupthink occurs, members quickly agree on solutions, and those who dissent are ignored or removed from the group. This happened within President Kennedy's National Security Council during the Bay of Pigs deliberations. Arthur Schlesinger was told by Robert Kennedy to keep his objections to himself. The attorney general remarked: "You may be right or you may be wrong, but the president has made his mind up. Don't push it any further. Now is the time for everyone to help him all they can."[30] From that point on, Schlesinger never publicly dissented from the majority opinion, although he did so in his private communications.

When groupthink occurs, members believe that they are beyond error or reproach. Often they ignore any evidence that could threaten the group's "apparent" consensus by either attacking its source or its sponsor. We say apparent consensus because often if the group members were polled privately, many would still have serious reservations. Yet they withhold their reservations from one another in the mistaken belief that they are the only ones with lingering doubts. I once dealt with a five-member group in which three members did not agree with the apparent consensus. How is it possible for a group of five to have a consensus when three members have reservations? Apparent consensus yes, real consensus no!

Groupthink destroys critical thinking. Members ignore warnings and data that are counter to the group's apparent consensus. We see this behavior taken to an extreme during the Bay of Pigs planning meetings. Let us examine some claims that went unchallenged during the deliberations (Exhibit 2-8).

EXHIBIT 2-8
When Groupthink Operates

Claim	Reality
No one will know that the U.S. is involved in the invasion. Most people will believe the CIA story.	There were stories of the training camps in Guatemala in the newspapers.
Cuban Air Force can be neutralized.	The invasion force's B26 aircraft were obsolete and had frequent engine trouble.
There is high morale within the brigade. They will fight without U.S. ground troops.	One month before the attack there was a mutiny. The CIA told the brigade that they would not be allowed to fail.
Castro's army is weak. The brigade will be able to establish a beachhead.	Intelligence reported that the Cuban army was effective. Within one day of the landing, 20,000 Cuban troops surrounded the brigade.
If the landing fails, the brigade can escape to Escambray Mountains.	The brigade was not trained in guerrilla warfare. Escape option was only possible for the original landing site. Between the Bay of Pigs and the mountains was 80 miles of jungle and swamps. Did anyone look at a map of Cuba?

Finally, when groupthink occurs, the group develops and promotes negative stereotypes of outsiders or of nonconforming group members. An excellent illustration was the reaction of Admiral Kimmel's staff at Pearl Harbor prior to World War II. The group was repeatedly warned that Japanese aircraft carriers could not be sighted, and that this might be a prelude to a surprise attack on Pearl Harbor. Kimmel's staff labeled Japan as a "midget nation" that would not dare attack the mighty United States.[31]

In summary, groupthink operates when a premature consensus-at-all-costs mentality pervades a team's deliberation. Outsiders are viewed as weak or immoral and incapable of action, self-censorship occurs, dissent is privately rationalized, and there is pressure on dissenters to accept the *apparent* majority's beliefs and actions.

SUMMARY

Groups fail because of individual and group pathologies. Individuals bring all their weaknesses to the group. We are not the judgment makers we ought to be. We are subject to many heuristics that rob us of our problem-solving effectiveness. But even if we were all-wise and all-knowing, groups would still fail because we do not know how to effectively lead them. Failures in group dynamics and groupthink produce process losses that may overwhelm the native intelligence of the group's members. Groups often exhibit the "goldilocks syndrome." They can have too little or too much cohesion; too little or too much conflict; or be too small or too large. What is just right is not always easy to know. Group problem solving is as much an art as it is a science. In the next chapter we examine what can be done to overcome these individual and group pathologies that keep groups from realizing their potential.

ENDNOTES

1. Irving Janis, *Groupthink: Psychological Studies of Policy Decisions and Fiascoes*, 2nd ed. (Boston: Houghton Mifflin, 1982).

2. Arthur Elstein et al., "Methods and Theory in the Study of Medical Inquiry," *Journal of Medical Education* 47, no. 2 (1972): 85–92.

3. Ernest Alexander, "The Design of Alternatives in Organizational Contexts," *Administrative Science Quarterly* 24, no. 3 (1979): 382–404.

4. Randy Y. Hirokawa and Rodger Pace, "A Descriptive Investigation of the Possible Communication-Based Reasons for Effective and Ineffective Group Decision Making," *Communication Monographs* (December 1983): 363–80.

5. L. Richard Hoffman, "Improving the Problem Solving Process in Managerial Groups," in *Improving Group Decision Making in Organizations*, ed. Richard Guzzo (New York: Academic Press, 1982).

6. Harvey J. Brightman, *Problem Solving: A Logical and Creative Approach* (Atlanta: Business Publishing Division, Georgia State University, 1980).

7. Adapted with permission from *Managing Group Creativity* by Arthur VanGundy (New York: AMA, 1984), 54–57.

8. Arthur VanGundy, *Managing Group Creativity* (New York: AMACOM, 1984), 54–57.

9. DeWitt C. Dearborn and Herbert A. Simon, "Selective Perception: A Note on the Departmental Identifications of Executives," *Sociometry* 21 (1958): 140–44.

10. F. C. Bartlett, *Remembering* (London: Cambridge University Press, 1932), 171–76.

11. Harvey J. Brightman, "The Attack on Pearl Harbor: A Decision Science Perspective" (Paper presented at the annual meeting of the Decision Sciences Institute, Honolulu, Hawaii, November 1986).

12. United States Congress, *Pearl Harbor Attack, Hearings Before the Joint Committee on the Investigation of the Pearl Harbor Attack*, 79th Congress, Public Document #79716 (Washington: Government Printing Office, 1946).

13. Gordon Prange, *At Dawn We Slept* (New York: McGraw Hill, 1981), 36.

14. Ibid., 585.

15. Paul Slovic, *Toward Understanding and Improving Decisions* (Eugene, Oregon: Decision Research, 1981).

16. Malcolm Bradbury, "The Institutional Joneses," *Punch*, 10 February 1960.

17. James Gibson, John Ivancevich, and James Donnelly, Jr. *Organizations' Behavior, Structure, Processes*, 3rd ed. (Dallas: Business Publications Inc., 1979), 409.

18. J. Forester, "Status Race," *London Observer Colour Magazine*, 5 December 1965.

19. Michael Finigan, "The Effects of Token Representation on Participation in Small Decision Making Groups," *Economic and Industrial Democracy* 3 (1982): 531-50.

20. M. D. Pugh and R. Wahrman, "Neutralizing Sexism in Mixed-Sex Groups: Do Women Have to be Better than Men?" *American Journal of Sociology* 88, no. 4 (1983): 746-52.

21. Paul Watzlawick, *How Real is Real?* (New York: Random House, 1976), 66.

22. Robert M. Krauss, "Language as a Symbolic Process in Communication," *American Scientist* (Autumn 1968): 265-78.

23. Alvin F. Zander, *Making Groups Effective* (San Francisco: Jossey-Bass, 1982), 34.

24. Phillip Yetton and Preston C. Bottger, "The Relationships Among Group Size, Member Ability, Social Decision Schemes, and Performance," *Organization Behavior and Human Performance*, 32, no. 2 (1983): 145-59.

25. Alvin F. Zander, *Making Groups Effective*, 6.

26. Irving Janis, *Victims of Groupthink* (Boston: Houghton Mifflin, 1972).

27. Irving Janis, *Groupthink: Psychological Studies of Policy Decisions and Fiascoes* (Boston: Houghton Mifflin, 1982), 244.

28. Andrew H. Van De Ven and Andre L. Debecq, "The Effectiveness of Nominal, Delphi, and Interacting Group Decision-Making Processes," *The Academy of Management Journal* 17, no. 4 (1974): 605-21.

29. Isabel Briggs Myers and Mary H. McCaulley, *Manual: A Guide to the Development and Use of the Myers-Briggs Type Indicator* (Palo Alto, California: Consulting Psychologist Press, 1985).

30. Janis, *Victims of Groupthink*, 42.

31. Ibid., 87.

THREE

GENERAL STRATEGIES *for* IMPROVING TEAM EFFECTIVENESS

In this chapter we examine some general strategies for improving team performance. You will learn to (1) overcome some common heuristics, (2) improve your group leadership skills, and (3) run more effective team meetings. In the process, you will come to understand how you solve problems and make decisions—your decision-making style. The chapter concludes with an overview of my constructive conflict team problem-solving model.

OVERCOMING HEURISTICS

Knowing that we use heuristics is the first step in overcoming them. In diagnosing a problem you now know that selective perception may cause others to see the problem differently. You are more likely to avoid availability and base judgments solely on your ability to recall instances from memory. You are less likely to place greater weight on concrete and personal data over abstract data sources. In short, you know how to avoid judgmental traps. But there are some specific methods for overcoming particular heuristics, and we turn to these next.

Overcoming Selective Perception

Selective perception is the tendency to view problems from our own unique perspective. Our view of a problem is colored by our life experiences, education, and personality. What we see depends not only on what is out there, but on who we are. The danger is that we begin to believe that there is only one way to view a problem—ours—and that everybody else is wrong.

There are two strategies for minimizing selective perception. First, consider forming heterogeneous teams. Perhaps the Pearl Harbor debacle could have been avoided if General Short's subordinates had not been clones of the general—if only Colonel Phillips had challenged Short's interpretation of the war warning message. While all of Short's officers were highly competent, they tended to share the general's view. There were no checks and balances to reality-test his thinking. In this and the next chapters we will discuss how to form heterogeneous teams.

Second, your team may also use the Alternative Worldview diagnostic tool. This technique helps you analyze a problem from different perspectives or angles. The purpose is to force team members to consider alternative causes to a complex problem. The Alternative Worldview Method will be presented in Chapter 5.

Overcoming Availability, Statistical Regression, Concreteness

These three heuristics—*availability, statistical regression,* and *concreteness*—happen when team members do not subject others' beliefs or claims to rigorous scrutiny. They accept what other team members say without demanding "where's the evidence?" You can minimize these three heuristics by using the following Rational Argumentation Model:[1]

We all have difficulty in distinguishing facts from claims. As someone once said, "If you say it, it is a claim: if I say it, it is a fact." The Rational Argumentation Model demands that all statements made during a group meeting be treated as claims, in search of supporting evidence.

When you make a statement (claim) you must present supporting *data.* Who or what says that your claim is correct? Why should I believe you? Where is the evidence? The *warrants* tell other team members why they should accept your data as supporting the claim. Warrants are rules, principles, and premises that act as a bridge between the data and the claim. Because members often do not explicitly state them, warrants must be inferred by the other team members. The *rebuttal* provides a safety valve for the argument. It states the conditions under which the claim may not be true. It helps to qualify and assess the claim's plausibility.

Here is how you should present a claim:

First—*Claim*

Second—*Data*—read as "given"

Third—*Warrant*—read as "because"

Fourth—*Rebuttal*—read as "unless"

In Chapter 2 we discussed how a senior management team within a drug firm dealt with a significant threat to a major product. The firm was considering raising the price to combat the competition. A senior team member had argued that doctors would continue to recommend the drug even if the price were raised. He personally believed that doctors were price insensitive.

Here are two possible sets of data, warrants, and rebuttals for the claim that doctors are price insensitive:

Claim: Doctors will continue to prescribe our drug.

Argument 1		Argument 2	
Data:	Given my recent talk with my brother-in-law, who is a doctor.	*Data:*	Given the results of a recent market research survey.
Warrant:	Because my brother-in-law is always correct on these issues.	*Warrant:*	Because the sample was representative and the research group has done good work before.
Rebuttal:	Unless my brother-in-law is not representative of all doctors. And he may not be, for he is an "uptown" doctor.	*Rebuttal:*	Unless the recent hearing on health legislation has caused an opinion shift.

Compare and contrast both arguments. In Argument 1, our claim maker is suffering from the concreteness heuristic. The team can evaluate the claim based on its logic rather than on the presenter's status.

When you use the Rational Argumentation Model, others can determine the plausibility of your claim. Unfortunately, most of us do not present our claims this way. Rather we state them as facts, and others often naively accept them. Remember, facts don't exist—only claims in search of evidence.

Effective groups may not always use the Rational Argumentation Model, but they do examine the validity of opinions and assumptions.[2] Ineffective groups rarely challenge others and treat opinions as facts. The lesson is clear: *Use rational argumentation.*

Overcoming Representativeness

Managers use the representativeness heuristic when they ignore *base rate* data in making estimates. Rather they make their estimates using only *representativeness* data in violation of the principles of statistical reasoning. You must use both types of data in estimating probabilities.

Here we consider a simple graphic method for combining the two types of data. Let's apply it to the problems presented in Chapter 2.

Seismic Test Problem: Before a well is drilled, oil companies frequently conduct seismic tests. The less-than-perfect test indicates that oil is likely or unlikely. Here is the representativeness data:

> Of those wells where we found oil, 70% of the tests had indicated that oil was likely. Of those wells where we didn't find oil, 75% of the tests had indicated that oil was not likely.

Previously you were not given the base rate data and could not solve the problem. The base rate data is the probability of finding oil in the oil field no matter what the outcome of the seismic test is. Let us assume that the base rate probability is 20%. By that I mean that 20% of all wells have struck oil. Now you can determine the chances of striking oil if the seismic test says that oil is likely.

Imagine there are 200 oil wells in the field. The actual number is irrelevant. Choose a round number to keep the subsequent math simple. First apply the base rate data to the 200 wells. We know that we found oil in 20% (.20 × 200) or 40 wells. This means that there were 160 dry wells:

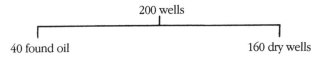

200 wells

40 found oil   160 dry wells

Now apply the representativeness data first to the 40 wells that found oil and then to the 160 dry wells. Of the 40 producing wells, we know that in 70% (.70 × 40) or 28 wells the seismic test had said that oil was likely. Thus in 12 (40 − 28) wells, the seismic test said that oil was unlikely. Of the 160 dry wells, we know that in 75% (.75 × 160) or 120 wells the seismic test had said that oil was unlikely. Thus in 40 (160 − 120) wells, the seismic test said that oil was likely. I've captured all this information in the following tree diagram:

200 wells

40 found oil   *160 dry*

| Seismic test says oil is likely in 28 | Seismic test says oil is unlikely in 12 | Seismic test says oil is likely in 40 | Seismic test says oil is unlikely in 120 |

What is the probability of finding oil if the seismic test had said that oil was likely? The denominator of the desired probability is the number of wells in which the seismic test had said that oil was likely. There are 68 wells (28 + 40). Of those 68 wells, we actually found oil in 28. Therefore the desired probability is 28/68 = .41 or 41%.

Most people guesstimate around 70%—very close to the representativeness data. The fact is that we are lousy intuitive statisticians!

The Computer Scanning Problem. A computer company uses a scanning device that places a mark on each defective chip it spots in the production line. The quality control department reports that 20% of all chips are defective—the base rate data. Here is the representativeness data:

> When a chip is okay, the scanner correctly leaves it unmarked 90% of the time. When a chip is defective, the scanner marks it as defective 90% of the time.

First, apply the base rate data. This time let's assume 1,000 chips. Of the 1,000 chips, 20% (.20 × 1,000) or 200 chips are defective. That leaves 800 okay chips. Now apply the representativeness data to the 200 defective and the 800 okay chips. When a chip is okay, the scanner leaves it unmarked 90% of the time. Of the 800 okay chips, the scanner will leave 720 (800 × .9) unmarked. When a chip is defective, the scanner marks it as defective 90% of the time. Of the 200 defective chips, the scanner will mark 180 (200 × .9) as defective.

All the numbers are captured in the following tree diagram:

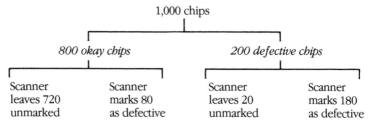

Now we can compute the chances that a computer chip is really defective if the scanner marks it as defective. The denominator of the desired probability is the number of chips that the scanner marked as defective. There are 260 marked chips (80 + 180).

Of the 260 chips, 180 were actually defective. Thus the desired probability is $180/260 = .69$ or 69%.

Without the tree diagram, most people guesstimate around 90%—very close to the representativeness data. That is because they succumbed to the representativeness heuristic. The tree diagram is an effective method for combining base rate and representativeness data to determine the desired probability.

In summary, first use the base rate data to divide the problem into two categories. For example, good and bad chips or dry and producing wells. Then apply the representativeness data to each of the two categories, and draw your tree diagram. Use it to determine the desired probability.

OVERCOMING GROUPTHINK

The empirical evidence in support of groupthink is not overpowering.[3] Perhaps the inconsistent findings are due to studying short-lived ad hoc groups. Can the level and quality of cohesion required for groupthink be achieved in such groups? As Irving Janis recently noted, there is cohesion, and then there is cohesion:

> Concurrence-seeking tendencies probably are stronger when high cohesiveness is based primarily on the rewards of being in a pleasant "clubby" atmosphere or of gaining prestige from being a member of an elite group rather than when it is based primarily on the opportunity to function competently on work tasks with effective co-workers.[4]

When the conditions for groupthink are present, consider using the following principles in leading a managerial problem-solving team. These draw heavily on the three sets of leadership skills— listening or clarifying, supporting or encouraging, and creating a constructive conflict environment (Chapter 2).

PRINCIPLE 1: *Critical thinking uber alles.*

To overcome self-censorship, encourage your team members to air their objections and doubts. But practice what you preach. We know that groups form norms, or operating rules, in the first few meetings. If a team member is ridiculed the first time he raises an objection, and you do nothing to protect him, the group members adopt a norm of "keep it to yourself."

How can you structure the group meetings or operations to get group members to open up? As leader you must demonstrate that you can be influenced by those who disagree with you. When others see this they will begin to open up, and you will establish a norm of critical thinking. You may also schedule special meetings in which group members can systematically raise concerns with the proposed alternatives. We call these second-look meetings. Also, consider setting-up special channels that allow members to share concerns in anonymity. These are especially useful when your team is working on a politically explosive problem.

You may find it difficult to encourage critical thinking in amiable and highly cohesive groups. After all, critical thinking can produce conflict. The members realize that sometimes critical thinking leads to damaged feelings, especially for those whose doubts are rejected or ignored. While that risk is real, critical thinking must overrule tranquility.

Too much conflict can occur when you have a group of curmudgeons who engage in prolonged debate without end. They continue to travel over old ground and to resurrect old arguments *ad nauseam.* This is not critical thinking; it is merely aggravation. As leader you must be ready to thank the group for their deliberations, and conclude the meeting.

PRINCIPLE 2: *Do not proselytize.*

In their initial presentation of a problem, team leaders often discuss what they believe are its causes and suggest or propose alternative solutions. Then they open the meeting up for general discussion. This is counterproductive and it can, consciously or subconsciously, lead to *anchoring*—once an idea is on the table, others may agree or disagree with it, but it is difficult to generate truly different ideas.

Present the facts of the problem and the time and dollar constraints under which the group must operate. But do not offer possible causes or alternative solutions. Remain nonevaluative at the outset. Do not try to sell your own pet theories. Let the team wrestle with the basic facts. Encourage each member to seek out multiple diagnoses of the problem and several alternative solutions.

However, do not wait forever to share your ideas. If you do, the group will lose a valuable information resource and team member. Do not proselytize but, rather, guide the group to explore the problem fully. Be a facilitator, not a director (Exhibit 3-1).

EXHIBIT 3-1
Two Styles of Group Leadership

Facilitator	Director
Agreement by collaboration	Agreement by exhaustion
Open-minded	Closed-minded
Free discussion	Focused discussion
Everyone participates	High-status members speak
Judge	Salesman
Present facts early	Present facts and conclusions early
Let's try for consensus—if not, I'll make the decision	For those who disagree, "Kick . . . and take names"

It takes an exceptional leader not to be frustrated when the group rambles on. Frustration can easily lead to "tightening the reins," and reinstituting a more directive team leadership style. Fight the feeling!

Here is what not to do (excerpt from an interview):

> In the meeting in which I was informed that I was released, I was told: Bill, in general, people who do well in this company wait until they hear their superiors express their views and then contribute something in support of that view.[5]

PRINCIPLE 3: *Use the devil's advocate.*

The oldest form of formalized dissent occurs within the Roman Catholic Church. The devil's advocate has been a continuing office since the early 1500s. The office thoroughly investigates proposals for canonization and beatification. The devil's advocate must bring to light any information that would cast doubt on the candidate for sainthood. The underlying assumption is that the best decisions can be made by separating the functions of promoter and dissenter.

In the business world, the devil's advocate role is to find fault with the group's current thinking—a diagnosis, an alternative, or an implementation plan. The advocate must force the group to surface its underlying claims or assumptions and challenge them. The devil's advocate should use the Rational Argumentation Model presented previously, demand the data and warrants behind a position, and construct careful rebuttals. Over time the advocate can help others to use the Rational Argumentation Model.

Assign the devil's advocate role to one or two members on a rotating basis. Two members are better than one (especially in larger groups) because a serious advocate can upset other group members. They may know intellectually that the advocate is only playing an important role. Nevertheless, when your arguments are repeatedly challenged, your frustration level rises, and you may attempt to "punish" the advocate.

During the Cuban Missile Crisis, President Kennedy assigned his brother the devil's advocate role.[6] He was very good. In fact he may have been too good, for it cost him a considerable amount of popularity among his colleagues. Had he not been the president's brother, his political career might have been ruined. When there are two advocates, they can share the heat and provide moral support for one another. One final note: as group leader you must protect the devil's advocate from the verbal abuse of others. Otherwise, the advocate will only "go through the motions."

Rotate the devil's advocate role among some, if not all, team members. This will avoid the advocate becoming domesticated. From time-to-time the role needs to be regenerated and given new vitality. Domesticated devil's advocates create a false sense of security. The group may believe that the advocate has forced it to analyze all the issues when, in fact, the advocate has been a paper tiger. Furthermore, by having many, if not all, members be devil's advocates, you create a constructive conflict climate.

Eventually all members will be able to air objections and doubts in a professional, not personal, manner.

PRINCIPLE 4: *Everyone participates.*

Everyone should participate in a team meeting. When only high-status members speak, problem solving deteriorates. Encourage your more introverted, junior, or female team members to participate. Full participation is especially needed under crisis or high-stress conditions. Yet we know that under extreme time and stress conditions, groups restrict communication and "close their borders."[7] However, even full participation does not ensure that all team members will think critically.

You need a group structure that requires all members to think and participate during a group's deliberations.

PRINCIPLE 5: *Reality-test ideas.*

Often groups that are either physically or psychologically isolated lose touch with reality. They have no way of reality-testing their ideas. Consider bringing trusted associates into your group on a short-term basis. They may be able to detect unseen flaws in your analysis. Alternatively, you can bring in internal or external experts to review your ideas.

Be aware of the potential for breach of security. The more people who are involved in the deliberations, the greater is the risk of a leak.

PRINCIPLE 6: *Have a second-look meeting.*

Ineffective groups often reject alternative solutions before fully discussing them.[8] We call this *preformal closure.* You can minimize preformal closure by calling a second-look meeting after you have reached an apparent consensus. Now reconsider your action. Alfred Sloan, a former chairman of General Motors, followed this plan:

> Gentlemen, I take it we are all in complete agreement on the decision here. . . . Then I propose we postpone further discussion of this matter until our next meeting to give ourselves time to develop disagreement and perhaps gain some understanding of what the decision is all about.[9]

A second-look meeting serves two purposes:

1. To compare and contrast earlier discarded actions with the selected alternative.

2. To analyze potential problems. Imagine that you have implemented your chosen alternative. What problems are you likely to encounter as you implement the solution? What countermeasures will you need to overcome these implementation problems? We call this *potential problem analysis.*

Teams often reject alternatives without subjecting them to a formal analysis. A senior person may react negatively to an idea, and the group immediately drops it from discussion. In the second-look meeting resurrect these ideas and compare them to the chosen alternative. This comparison serves two purposes. It ensures that the chosen alternative is really best. It also improves the chances of getting a solution approved by demonstrating the team's thoroughness to the decision authorizers.

Murphy was an optimist—whatever can go wrong, must go wrong. When people believe that a solution will cause major changes in the organization, they follow one of three strategies—accept or embrace it, fight it, or ignore it. If they choose to fight, your team must be ready to respond by developing strategies or tactics that will counter the counter-implementors' efforts. A second-look meeting provides such an opportunity.

PRINCIPLE 7: *Group, know thyself!*

Groups often get so involved in solving problems that they do not examine how they do it.[10] On a regular basis, groups should set aside time to examine their own internal problem-solving processes.[11] What did we do right? What did we do wrong? And how will we improve? In short, teams need to critique themselves. It is inevitable that teams will make mistakes.

It is unforgivable if they make the same problem-solving mistakes again and again. Do review and improve!

Consider using the questionnaire in Exhibit 3-2 to critique your group's operations.[12] Have your team members complete the questionnaire anonymously.

In summary, use the following principles and you will reduce the chance of groupthink:

1. Critical thinking uber alles
2. Don't proselytize
3. Use the devil's advocate
4. Everyone participates
5. Reality-test ideas
6. Have a second-look meeting
7. Group, know thyself

Some of these ideas need no further elaboration. Others will be discussed in subsequent chapters. Now we consider how to ensure that everyone participates in the team's deliberations.

THE NOMINAL GROUP TECHNIQUE

Andre Delbecq and Andrew Van De Ven's *Nominal Group Technique* produces higher quality alternatives, more accurate decisions or judgments, and stronger feelings of accomplishment than do free-flowing discussion groups.[13] Discussion groups have no formal rules or structures to organize or control members' participation. People speak when they have something to say; otherwise they remain quiet. Discussion groups have three major weaknesses: (1) inequality of participation, (2) group-think and self-censorship, and (3) the anchoring effect.

You are already familiar with the dangers of inequality of participation (Exhibit 2-8) and self-censorship. *Anchoring* further degrades problem-solving effectiveness. It occurs when a senior person prematurely discusses the causes of or alternative solutions to a problem. Once these ideas have been presented, others may agree or disagree, but team members will find it extremely difficult to generate new ideas.

(Text continued on page 73)

EXHIBIT 3-2

Team Process Critique Questionnaire

1. To what extent do I feel a real part of this team?

1	2	3	4	5
Completely a part at all times.		On the edge.		On the outside, not a part of the team.

2. How safe is it to be at ease, relaxed, and myself?

1	2	3	4	5
I feel very safe to be myself. Others won't hold mistakes against me.		You have to be careful what you say and do.		A person would have to be a fool to be himself.

3. To what extent do I feel "under wraps," that is, I have private thoughts or unexpressed feelings that I have not felt comfortable bringing out into the open?

1	2	3	4	5
Almost completely under wraps.		Somewhat expressive.		Almost completely free and expressive.

4. How effective are we in getting opinions and information from all team members in making decisions?

1	2	3	4	5
We don't really encourage sharing ideas and feelings.		Sometimes we share and sometimes we don't.		All ideas are given a free hearing before the decision is made.

5. To what extent are the team's goals understood and meaningful to me?

1	2	3	4	5
I feel extremely good about our team's goals.		I understand and am somewhat involved in the team's goals.		I do not understand or feel involved in the team's goals.

6. How well does the team work at its tasks?

1	2	3	4	5
Coasts—makes no progress.		Slow progress but spurts of effective work.		Works well and achieves definite progress.

(Continued)

7. Our planning and the way we operate as a team is largely influenced by:

1	2	3	4	5
One or two team members.		Half the team members.		All members of the team.

8. What is the level of responsibility for work in our team?

1	2	3	4	5
Each person assumes responsibility for getting work done.		Half and half.		Nobody, except maybe me, assumes responsibility.

9. How are differences handled within the group?

1	2	3	4	5
They are denied, suppressed, or avoided at all costs.		Some attempt to work them out— often outside the meeting.		Differences are recognized and are usually worked out satisfactorily.

Source: Adapted with permission from *The Guided Design Handbook: Patterns of Implementation* by William Coscarelli and Gregory White (Morgantown, West Virginia: National Center for Guided Design, 1986), 141–43.

(Continued from page 69)

Perhaps an analogy will clarify the anchoring concept. Let us equate drilling for oil with problem solving. Finding oil is equivalent to solving the problem. A senior person's initial idea can be represented as a deep shaft into the ground:

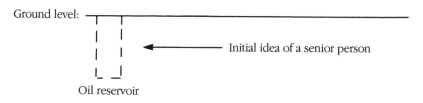

Ground level:

Initial idea of a senior person

Oil reservoir

When a senior person speaks, team members *listen* and *react.* Thus they can find it very difficult to start digging shafts (or generating alternative solutions) far away from the initial drilling site. It is as if the initial idea *anchors* all subsequent discussion. If the oil is located as shown in the illustration, the group will find it (and solve the problem). But if the oil is located far from the initial shaft, the problem may never be solved. Discussion groups usually have one idea generator (the senior person) and multiple idea reactors (junior personnel). Effectiveness increases when all members generate ideas.

Continuing with our analogy, what we want are multiple initial shafts in the ground. Thus, no matter where the oil is, we will find it. The Nominal Group Technique generates multiple initial positions, provides for more equal participation within the group, and minimizes the possibility of self-censorship.

Here are the five steps of the Nominal Group Technique:

Initial Thoughts. Group members silently and independently generate their diagnoses or alternative solutions. This can even be done before the meeting starts. Do not allow any intra-group discussion.

Round-robin. Each member now presents an analysis. Do not discuss or criticize the presentations. Permit only questions of clarification. The team leader can make a presentation, but should go last. Also ask group members to write and hand in their ideas.

Idea Structuring. Now team members rewrite the ideas to ensure that they are all at the same level of detail. You must compare "apples to apples." When the team has generated a large number of ideas, consider clustering them into a few mega-ideas. Assign subgroups of two or more people to each idea cluster to further develop the ideas prior to the discussion phase.

Discussion and Synthesis. Help the group explore and compare all the ideas. Differences must be examined, not ignored. Summarize frequently and ensure that all ideas are discussed, especially those authored by junior or introverted team members. Handle conflicts in a collaborative manner. Be assertive in presenting your ideas and listen to others' ideas. Strive for a synthesis that incorporates the best of each idea.

Closure. Try to reach a consensus. If this is not possible, have the group rank-order all the remaining ideas under discussion. Use a silent ballot.

Initial Thoughts—Phase 1

Every team member should analyze the problem without any outside interference. Each of us is different. We bring different experiences and educational backgrounds to a problem. If given a chance to analyze the problem independently, we are likely to generate different causes or alternative solutions. Do not allow members to communicate before developing their initial positions.

The team leader should present the basic facts of the problem, then ask each member to analyze its causes. The leader can also ask each member to develop an initial presentation before the group meeting. This saves precious meeting time. However, sometimes think-type assignments are forgotten in the press of day-to-day activities. If you ask your team members to prepare before a meeting, warn them not to discuss their positions with one another. Why? Because if you tell me your idea, I might decide, in a split instant, that it is better than mine. Now the team will never hear my idea. Moreover, all variations of my original idea may also be lost. This is self-censorship at its worst.

Round-robin—Phase 2

Next, we get all the ideas on the table. Everyone makes a presentation. Its length depends on the available time. It can be 30 seconds (for a crisis problem) to an hour (for a strategic problem). Presentations can range from handwriting on easel pad paper to 35mm slides or computer video presentations. Remember to allocate time for the first two phases commensurate with your time constraints.

Allow only questions of clarification. The natural tendency is for opposing sides to argue about one idea before all the ideas have been presented. As psychologist Norman Maier noted, we are solution-minded managers.[14] Allowing a detailed discussion on one idea before all have been presented is equivalent to digging one deep shaft before other wells have been sunk. This defeats the purpose of the Nominal Group Technique. Do not allow the group to analyze any argument until all have been presented.

Perhaps the two most difficult issues are (1) who should present first? and (2) should the team leader make a presentation? In most discussion groups, higher status members monopolize the conversation, that is, "status speaks." To overcome this, the most junior status member should make the first presentation. The last presenter should be the team's highest-ranking member. In this way you eliminate the possibility of a situation I once observed. A firm's CEO had decided to use the Nominal Group Technique for his staff meetings. He asked his staff members to come to the monthly meeting prepared with presentations on a tough problem. A very senior person (not the CEO) spoke first. As he made his presentation, a junior staff member crumpled up his paper and put it in his coat pocket. When it came time for his presentation he responded, "My ideas are the same as Dick's (the senior person)." Remember, junior personnel may initially feel uncomfortable in presenting radically different ideas. But you must not allow self-censorship. Of course, had the CEO seen what had happened and encouraged the junior person to make his original presentation, the norm of "everyone says what's on their mind" would have been established. Remember, have the junior people speak first.

Should the team leader make a presentation? If he or she

does not, then members will be free to explore their options without any psychological interference. By not making a presentation the team leader is expressing confidence in the team's ability to solve the problem. This strategy is especially useful when team members tend to over-rely on the team leader's input. During the Cuban missile crisis, President Kennedy was so concerned that the National Security Council would echo his line that he kept his thoughts to himself. On the other hand, if the team leader does not make a presentation, the team has lost an important resource. The leader's presentation may provide insight and information that is not readily available from other sources. Perhaps you should not make a presentation the first several times you use the Nominal Group Technique. Thereafter, you should make the last presentation in the round-robin.

The normal procedure is for each person to make their own opening argument. When you want to divorce the presenters from their ideas, consider the following two variations. Have one person make all the opening arguments. This individual need not even be a member of the group. Now all the ideas can be evaluated on their merits because during the critical initial impression stage, the "status speaks" bias will be muted.

Alternatively, you may use *ringii*, a Japanese decision-making procedure.[15] Instead of making oral presentations, each person's initial idea is passed around to all other members in the group. Members write comments on each idea and continue to circulate the drafts until no more changes are made. Now the group is ready to discuss all the ideas.

Make sure that all ideas are written and handed in to the team leader. This ensures that none of the ideas will "fall through the cracks" during the subsequent phases. Even if introverted junior team members do not pursue their ideas, they will not be forgotten. Moreover, you can compare these ideas with the selected alternative at the second-look meeting. The spoken thought is ephemeral, the written word endures.

Idea Structuring—Phase 3

Structuring ensures that all ideas are at the same level of detail and collapses many ideas into a few. Unless ideas are at the same level of detail, they are difficult to evaluate fairly. And we expect that ideas will be at different levels of specificity. Some of us like to provide specific details in our initial ideas while others believe that too many details smother the big picture. You will need to expand brief ideas and abridge complicated ideas to ensure that all are at the same level of detail.

Often teams generate a very large number of similar ideas during the round-robin. You may want to cluster the ideas into a few mega-ideas that capture all the options. Recently a consulting firm used this clustering approach in developing an environmental strategy for coal-burning plants.[16] The project team initially generated the following 15 ideas during the round-robin:

1. Define chemical, physical, and toxicological properties to be used for comparison.

2. Develop large volume sampler.

3. Examine alteration of chemical and physical properties of particle samples during collection, storage, and resuspension.

4. Develop criteria for site selection and screen tests.

5. Develop extraction procedures.

6. Develop internal standards.

7. Develop collection techniques for fine particles in stack.

8. Develop adequate aerosol resuspension techniques.

9. Develop advanced analytical procedures for detail screening.

10. Develop other collection techniques.

11. Develop data base on relation of emission screening of samples.

12. Define protocols for chemical and toxicological screening of samples.

13. Develop sample recovery procedure.

14. Assess desirability of alternative collection strategy.

15. Develop laboratory combuster.

However, the group could not explore 15 ideas; there were simply too many. Each team member was given 15 cards, each containing one of the original ideas. The idea cards had wax backings so that team members could cluster them as they wished. The number of mega-ideas and the clustering of the original 15 ideas were left to each team member. Using a *silent and independent* process they agreed on four mega-ideas, as follows:

Develop Analytical Techniques	Develop Sample Handling Procedures
Idea 1	Idea 3
Idea 5	Idea 8
Idea 6	
Idea 9	
Idea 12	

Develop Collection Techniques	Site Selection
Idea 2	Idea 4
Idea 7	Idea 11
Idea 10	
Idea 13	
Idea 14	
Idea 15	

The four mega-ideas helped focus the discussion, and the group completed its analysis quickly.

Idea clustering is especially useful when the problem is complex or when many ideas are generated during the round-robin. Omit this step for crisis problems or when only a few ideas are generated.

Discussion and Synthesis—Phase 4

The key is to compare and contrast the ideas. Remember, to run an effective discussion you should:

- Strive for critical thinking.
- Avoid proselytizing your own ideas.
- Use the devil's advocate method.
- Ensure that everyone participates.
- Reality-test the group's ideas.

Productive team meetings happen when team members examine the validity of opinions and claims and are more rigorous in evaluating solutions. Team members should compare solutions to the stated goals and base their decisions on reasonable facts, inferences, and assumptions. They should ask questions, point out important information, or challenge the group to reject wrong arguments. Influential members are *facilitators*.

These are your goals during the fourth phase of the Nominal Group Technique.

Closure—Phase 5

Teams achieve closure in one of three ways. They (1) choose one of the original ideas (or a slight modification); (2) select the best elements from several ideas and develop a synthesis; or (3) generate a novel option. In the spirit of collaboration and compromise, teams often achieve a synthesis. Now everyone feels ownership of the option. Creative options occur because once team members discover that others have different ideas during the round-robin, they are open to new ideas. They use the initial options as a staging ground for creating new alternatives.

When the group fails to reach a consensus, the group leader can ask the members to rank order the remaining alternatives under discussion. Of course, the procedure is by silent ballot. In this way the team leader determines which options have the strongest support.

It is always fascinating to see groups develop creative solutions during the open-ended discussion of Phase 4. While the Nominal Group Technique aids the creative process, individual team members possess different levels of creativity. We explore these and other individual differences as we turn to decision-making style.

DECISION-MAKING STYLE

We know that individuals differ. But are there systematic differences between people? Carl Jung, one of the great minds of the twentieth century, believed that people could be differentiated along two different basic orientations and four psychological functions.[17]

The psychological functions tell us how people perceive and make judgments. They perceive through *sensing* or *intuition.* Sensors focus on the details and facts of the immediate experience. Intuitors see beyond what is visible. They draw hunches, find a pattern in seemingly unrelated events, or make a creative discovery. People make judgments through *thinking* or *feeling.*

Thinkers are analytical and link ideas logically to one another. Feelers allow personal values to influence their judgments. People also have different orientations toward life. Some focus on either the outside world of action and people (*extroverts*) or the inside world of ideas and thought (*introverts*).

Jung rejected the idea that we can use all four psychological functions equally well—we are not psychologically ambidextrous. Such impartiality keeps all the functions undeveloped and produces a "primitive mentality."[18] Whatever that is, it doesn't sound good! Jung believed that we are predisposed to use two of the psychological functions (one perception and one judgment function) over the others. As a result, we develop and become more skilled at these functions. These are our *dominant* and *auxiliary* functions. We have the most confidence in the dominant function, and therefore use it most frequently. The auxiliary, or helper, supports the dominant function. The remaining two functions are not developed and atrophy over time. For simplicity, these are called the inferior functions.

By early adulthood, each of us has a definite decision-making style. And we will probably not change. The two basic attitudes and four psychological functions combine to produce eight decision-making styles:

Extrovert with sensing dominant	E**S**T or E**S**F
Introvert with sensing dominant	I**S**T or I**S**F
Extrovert with intuition dominant	E**N**T or E**N**F
Introvert with intuition dominant	I**N**T or I**N**F
Extrovert with thinking dominant	ES**T** or EN**T**
Introvert with thinking dominant	IS**T** or IN**T**
Extrovert with feeling dominant	ES**F** or EN**F**
Introvert with feeling dominant	IS**F** or IN**F**

Note: The dominant function is bold-faced. The auxiliary is the other *psychological* function. For example, an E**S**T manager's dominant function is sensing and the auxiliary function is thinking. Intuition and feeling are the inferior functions.

During mid-life we gain greater control over the inferior functions. Nevertheless, we still rely on the dominant and, to a lesser extent, the auxiliary function for our entire life.

Basic Orientation: Extroversion or Introversion

This preference tells us where we go to get our energy and charge our batteries. Introverts (I) find energy in the inner world of ideas, concepts, and abstractions. They can be sociable but need to be by themselves to recharge their batteries. Introverted managers have trouble remembering names and faces, like to work on only one project, like to think a lot before acting, and are careful with details. Introverts are *concentrators.*

Extroverts (E) find energy in things and people. They are pulled by the outside world and are action-oriented. Extroverted managers like variety and action, are good at greeting people, don't mind answering the phone, and often act too quickly. Extroverts are *interactors.*

The extrovert's ideal vacation is to be with a group of people and friends. The destination is less important than the group. Introverts prefer to be by themselves. You might even be able to tell an extrovert from an introvert by the pictures they take. Extroverts take pictures of people; introverts take pictures of scenery and objects.

Psychological Function of Perception

This dimension focuses on how we collect data when making a decision. Some of us choose to rely on our five senses. Others prefer to use our sixth sense. Sensors (S) know something because they have experienced it directly through their five senses. They are detail-oriented, want facts, and trust them. Sensing managers like established routine, dislike problems unless they can be easily solved, and must work a problem all the way through to reach a conclusion.

Intuitors (N) seek out patterns and relationships between the facts they have gathered. They trust hunches and look at the big picture. Too much detail clutters up the problem. Intuitive managers like solving new problems, work in bursts of energy, are more creative, and frequently jump to conclusions.

A sensing personnel manager, in evaluating a prospective employee, looks at his past experiences, and determines the degree of fit between the applicant and the job. An intuitive personnel manager tries to visualize how the applicant will grow into the job. One looks to the future, the other to the past. There is no one best way; the managers are merely different.

Psychological Function of Judging

Once we have collected data, we are ready to make judgments. Some of us use analysis, logic, and principle to make judgments. Others personalize decisions and are concerned with their impact on people. Thinkers (T) value fairness. Thinking managers are uninterested in people's feelings, need to be treated fairly, and tend to relate well only to other thinking types. They focus on the logic of the situation and give greater weight to objective criteria. Their motto is: "If you can't quantify it, it doesn't count." Feeling (F) individuals value harmony. They focus on human values and needs as they make decisions or judgments. Feeling managers want harmony, dislike reprimanding subordinates, are good at resolving differences between colleagues, and let their decisions be influenced by other people's likes and wishes.

The abbreviated version of the Myers-Briggs Type Indicator (MBTI) is a reliable guide to your decision-making style.[19] Your score on the 50-item indicator consists of four letters (E or I, S or N, T or F, and a fourth dimension). The fourth dimension—Judging (J) or Perception (P)—is necessary to determine your dominant, auxiliary, and inferior functions.

Suppose the indicator tells you that you are an Introverted, iNtuitive, Thinking, Judging (INTJ) manager. One of your two psychological functions—Intuition (N) or Thinking (T)—will be your dominant function and the other will be your auxiliary function. Use Exhibit 3-3 to determine your decision-making style.

Your dominant function is Intuition (the intersection of the fourth column—NT—and first row—IJ). Thinking, the other psychological function, is your auxiliary, and sensing and feeling are your inferior functions. Since you are an Introvert, your decision-making style is Introvert with Intuition dominant. In short, you are an Introverted Intuitive.

Implications for Problem Solving

Jung's framework focuses on how people's apparently random behaviors are actually consistent when it comes to how they

EXHIBIT 3-3
Determining Your Dominant Function and Decision-Making Style

Dimensions #1 and #4 from MBTI	Dimensions #2 and #3 from MBTI			
	ST	*SF*	*NF*	*NT*
I–J	Sensing	Sensing	Intuition	Intuition
I–P	Thinking	Feeling	Feeling	Thinking
E–P	Sensing	Sensing	Intuition	Intuition
E–J	Thinking	Feeling	Feeling	Thinking

prefer to get their information, make decisions, and orient their lives. When people are aware of their differences in perception and judgment, they can reduce conflict and build on their differences. Decision-making style offers people a way to build communication patterns that will meet their needs as well as the needs of others. This allows them to be more effective in getting their ideas heard and implemented.

The model also offers us insight into our individual problem-solving strengths and weaknesses. Let us begin by meeting the perfect problem solver:

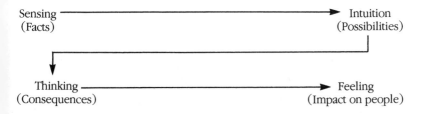

The perfect problem solver would use both sensing and intuition. Intuition, looking for connections and possibilities, depends on detailed data obtained by the sensing function. The perfect problem solver would then analytically examine intuited connections and possibilities, determine cause-effect relationships, and make a decision. The perfect problem solver would then use the feeling function to personalize the decision and to assess its impact on those involved.

Alas, we are not perfect problem solvers; we are mere mortals. We favor the dominant and auxiliary functions. These two functions are more fully engaged and have more influence in our problem-solving processes. We spend the least amount of time using our inferior functions. These are our blind spots. We must either (1) work at improving these functions or (2) assign key subordinates to cover our blind spots.

Improving inferior functions means learning new ways to solve problems. If you are sensing dominant, your creative potential has been dormant. To be creative, you must learn some creative problem-solving tools. The question is, will you? Creative tools may seem "unnatural" to a sensing-dominant manager. However, if you do accept and learn them, you will dramatically improve your problem-solving ability.

No one can be a perfect problem solver. We all have blind spots. But your subordinates should not have the same blind spots that you do. Synergy is possible where there are differences. When all departmental or team members are alike, there are no checks and balances.

Decision-making style describes how we gather data, make judgments, and orient our lives. You can use it to form optimal problem-solving teams. Group formation is, however, only one activity within my constructive conflict problem-solving model. It is time to reintroduce the model (see Exhibit 1-2, Chapter 1) and briefly discuss other specific tools and techniques.

A CONSTRUCTIVE CONFLICT MODEL
OF TEAM PROBLEM SOLVING

Early Group Behaviors—Task 1

First you must decide who should be a team member. Given the potential for groupthink, the goal is to maximize team-member heterogeneity through the use of decision-making style or other factors. The team must also write a charter. What is the group's understanding of its task, the constraints—time and budget—it will operate under, its formal place within the organization, and how it will operate as a group? Additionally, groups that are formed to identify opportunities or potential problems now engage in *problem finding.*

Exhibit 3-4 presents several techniques for the three activities of Task 1. Creative tools are divergent and expand our possibilities. They help us generate multiple problem causes or alternative solutions. Critical-thinking tools are convergent and narrow our choices down to one cause or solution. The effective problem solver has both tools in his problem-solving toolkit.

EXHIBIT 3-4
Specific Techniques for Task 1, Early Group Behaviors

Desired outcome	Specific techniques	Type of technique
Form a group	Decision-making style mix	Creative/Divergent
	Multiple stakeholders	Creative/Divergent
	Include installers	Creative/Divergent
Construct a charter	Charter construction	Critical/Convergent
Find problems or opportunities	Pounds's Model	Creative/Divergent
	Problem finding	Creative/Divergent

Diagnosis and Alternative Generation—Task 2

Here the goal is to diagnose the problem and then generate alternative solutions. What is diagnosis? That depends on the type of problem you are facing. *Disturbance problems* are gaps between your present and historic or budgeted levels of performance. Diagnosing disturbance problems means assessing causes of the gap. Unfortunately, American managers are not very good diagnosticians.[20] *Entrepreneurial problems* are gaps between the present and a higher or desired level of performance. Here, clearly articulating or formulating decision goals is critical to problem-solving success. Sometimes this is a straightforward process. We know the goals, and we merely have to articulate them to others on the team. Sometimes, unless we reformulate the goals, we may not be able to solve the problem. Reformulating objectives can widen the search for effective alternatives.

Finally we generate many *skeletal* ideas, screen them, and then fully develop the best contenders. A skeletal idea can be written on a single page. It is an executive summary or overview. It should include a brief description of the idea, its rationale, and very rough estimates of the costs and benefits. You then must reduce your list of ideas to a manageable size. In Task 2, generate at least two different, fully developed alternative solutions for formal evaluation.

Diagnosis and alternative generation must be interconnected processes because the alternatives you generate depend on your view of the causes. Diagnosis and alternative generation are two sides of the same coin. As you reconsider causes you will generate new alternatives.

Exhibit 3-5 contains the specific techniques for the diagnosis and alternative generation phase.

Choice and Implementation—Task 3

Here the group chooses an alternative, develops an implementation plan, and installs the solution. This book avoids mathematical approaches for selecting the best alternative because managers will not use them. Rather, it presents several rigorous and logical methods for selecting among competing alternatives.

Then the group must develop an implementation and counter-implementation document. The former describes the steps required to successfully install an alternative. It covers who, when, where, and how. Sometimes there are individuals or groups—we call them counter-implementors—who overtly or covertly oppose an alternative solution. They may simply be uneasy about any change or they may believe that they will lose power or status. They will do their best to thwart the implementation. We must be ready to beat the counter-implementors at their own game. We must develop a counter counter-implementation plan. We must imagine that we have attempted to implement the solution. What can or will go wrong? What games will the counter-implementors play? What games can we play to beat them?

EXHIBIT 3-5
Specific Techniques for Task 2, Diagnosis and Generation

Desired outcome	Specific techniques	Type of technique
Analyze causes	Alternative Worldview Kepner and Tregoe Model	Creative/Divergent Critical/Convergent
Formulate decision goals	Problem Boundary Expansion 5 Ws Method	Creative/Divergent Creative/Divergent
Generate skeletal ideas	Nominal Group Technique Analogy	Creative/Divergent Creative/Divergent
Screen skeletal ideas	Nominal Group Technique Franklin's Moral Algebra	Critical/Convergent Critical/Convergent

Exhibit 3-6 contains the specific techniques for the choice and implementation phase.

EXHIBIT 3-6
Specific Techniques for Task 3, Choice and Implementation

Desired outcome	Specific techniques	Type of technique
Select an alternative	Matrix Weighting Assumption Surfacing	Critical/Convergent Critical/Convergent
A second-look meeting	Reality Testing Potential Problem Analysis	Critical/Convergent Creative/Divergent
Design an implementation plan	Gantt Chart Scenario Writing	Critical/Convergent Creative/Divergent

SUMMARY

Groups fail because of individual and group pathologies. You have learned how to overcome many of the heuristics that rob us of our critical-thinking powers by using either the Rational Argumentation Model or the tree diagram. To overcome the group pathologies, you have learned seven general principles and focused specifically on the Nominal Group Technique, an approach that permits all team members to participate in the group's deliberations.

You also have gained insight into your own decision-making style. Whatever your dominant function, you should appreciate what others who are different have to offer to the team problem-solving process.

Exhibits 3-4 through 3-6 provide an introduction and road map for the remainder of the book. We are now ready to journey through the Team Problem-solving Model.

ENDNOTES

1. Richard Mason and Ian Mitroff, *Challenging Strategic Planning Assumptions* (New York: John Wiley, 1981), 213–16.

2. Randy Y. Hirokawa and Rodger Pace, "A Descriptive Investigation of the Possible Communication-Based Reasons for Effective and Ineffective Group Decision Making," *Communication Monographs* (December 1983): 363–80.

3. M. L. Flowers, "A Laboratory Investigation of Janis's Groupthink Hypothesis," *Journal of Personality and Social Psychology* 35 (1977): 288–99; Carrie Leana, "A Partial Test of Janis' Groupthink Model: Effects of Group Cohesiveness and Leader Behavior on Defective Decision Making," *Journal of Management* 11, no. 5 (1985): 5–17; Michael Callaway and James Esser, "Groupthink: Effects of Cohesiveness and Problem Solving Procedures on Group Decision Making," *Social Behavior and Personality* 12, no. 2 (1984): 157–64.

4. Irving Janis, *Victims of Groupthink* (Boston: Houghton Mifflin, 1972), 247–48.

5. Andrew Grove, "How High-Output Managers Reach Agreement in a Know-How Business," *Management Review* (December 1983): 8–13.

6. Janis, *Victims of Groupthink*, 216.

7. Daniel Isenberg, "Some Effects of Time Pressure on Vertical Structure and Decision Making Accuracy in Small Groups," *Organizational Behavior and Human Performance* 27 (1981): 119-34.

8. Ernest Alexander, "The Design of Alternatives in Organizational Contexts," *Administrative Science Quarterly* 24, no. 3 (1979): 382-404.

9. Janis, *Victims of Groupthink*, 218-19.

10. Carolyn Smart and Ilan Vertinsky, "Design for Crisis Decision Units," *Administrative Science Quarterly* (December 1977): 640-57.

11. Randy Hirokawa, "A Comparative Analysis of Communication Patterns Within Effective and Ineffective Decision Making Groups," *Communication Monographs* (November 1980): 312-21.

12. William Coscarelli and Gregory White, *The Guided Design Handbook: Patterns of Implementation* (Morgantown, West Virginia: National Center for Guided Design, 1986), 141-43.

13. Andrew H. Van De Ven and Andre L. Debecq, "The Effectiveness of Nominal, Delphi, and Interacting Group Decision-Making Processes," *The Academy of Management Journal* 17, no. 4 (1974): 605-21; J. Murnighan, "Group Decision Making: What Strategies Should You Use? *Management Review* (February 1981): 55-62; Harvey Brightman, Danny Lewis, and Penny Verhoeven, "Nominal and Interacting Groups as Bayesian Information Processors," *Psychological Reports* 52 (1983): 101-102.

14. Norman R. F. Maier, *Problem Solving and Creativity in Individual and Groups* (Monterey, California: Brooks/Cole, 1970).

15. Alvin Zander, *Making Groups Effective* (San Franciso: Jossey-Bass, 1982), 22-23.

16. Stuart Hart, et al., "Managing Complexity Through Consensus Mapping: Technology for the Structuring of Group Decisions," *Academy of Management Review* 10, no. 3 (1985): 587-600.

17. Carl Jung, *Psychological Types* (London: Routledge and Kegan Paul, 1923), 549-55.

18. Ibid., 406.

19. Isabel Briggs Myers and Mary H. McCaulley, *Manual: A Guide to the Development and Use of the Myers-Briggs Type Indicator* (Palo Alto, California: Consulting Psychologist Press, 1985), 7. The MBTI can be purchased through Consulting Psychologist Press, Inc., Palo Alto, California.

20. Peter F. Drucker, "What We Can Learn from Japanese Management," *Harvard Business Review* (March-April 1971): 110–22.

FOUR

EARLY
GROUP
BEHAVIORS

In Chapter 2 you learned three basic skills needed to lead a team problem-solving effort—listening and clarifying, supporting and encouraging, and creating constructive conflict. Based on these skills, in Chapter 3 I proposed seven principles of team leadership. Perhaps the most essential one was "critical thinking uber alles." In this chapter you will learn how to foster a critical thinking attitude right from the start. It begins with selecting the right team members, developing a proper group charter, and seeking projects to improve your department's performance.

PROBLEMS IN REAL-WORLD PRACTICE

Why are teams ineffective? Their problems begin at the beginning. Few managers *explicitly* consider whether to solve a problem alone or to form a team. Yet there are specific guidelines. To review briefly, make the decision alone when time is limited and you have all the needed information. Consult with your subordinates before making a decision when you lack sufficient information and the problem is ill-structured. Form a problem-solving team when, in addition to these considerations, acceptance of the decision by your subordinates is critical. If your subordinates can be trusted to share the organizational goals of the problem, use a participative problem-solving team. Otherwise, form an information-sharing team.

A manager need not be exceptional in every way. But a team must be, for this is how it achieves synergy. Unfortunately, we do not give enough thought to team appointments. Who is available and who has the necessary expertise are often the only considerations. Clearly, these are important factors. However, developing a critical-thinking attitude requires going beyond availability or expertise.

When offered a new job, effective CEOs either form staffs that will cover and compensate for their perceived weaknesses, or they do not take the job.[1] Follow this practice when forming teams.

Team members can have different perceptions of their mission. I once asked members of a long-standing team to write a brief statement on the team's goals and objectives. Unexpectedly, they were not in total agreement. Some thought they would implement whatever solution they developed; others thought they were merely an advisory committee. One member thought that the team could redefine the problem posed by senior management. Others were sure they did not have this freedom. Is it any wonder that the team was failing? Effective teams share the same goals and have the same view of their mission.[2] Constructing a group charter is the best way to ensure a common purpose for long-standing teams.

The highest form of leadership is *problem finding*. Here you create a new direction or vision for your department or organization. Problem finding separates managers who do things right from leaders who do the right things. Too often, teams are formed to react to a problem situation, not to seek out new problems or challenges facing the company. We must shift from a reactive to a proactive leadership style. Problem-solving teams can promote a vision-creating leadership climate.

A reactive leadership style permeates many organizations.

In our merger study, we asked CEOs or merger team leaders how they became aware of potential acquisition candidates?[3] Did they systematically and proactively seek out acquisition candidates based on explicit acquisition guidelines? Or, did candidates seek them out? Did they investigate multiple acquisition candidates? And was the acquisition part of a systematic program based on formal and explicit guidelines or was it ad hoc and opportunistic?

Of the 12 firms in the study, 7 had developed explicit acquisition guidelines. They were more mature firms and had been involved in previous acquisition programs. However, 3 firms were not actively seeking acquisition candidates. Of the 5 firms with no acquisition guidelines, all were reactive. Thus, 8 firms were waiting for opportunity to knock rather than opening the door. In one instance, an acquiring company hesitated to purchase a wine firm until its major competitor had "blazed the trail." If our ancestors had followed this strategy in taming the West, we would all live in Saint Joseph, Missouri.

The lack of proactiveness also affected the number of candidates the acquiring firm analyzed. The 8 reactive firms each investigated a single acquisition candidate. The proactive acquisition firms tended to examine multiple candidates.

A reactive leadership climate threatens our survival as an industrial democracy. We are convergent, not divergent. We are cautious, not bold. We are risk averters, not risk takers. Perhaps one reason for this is that we have too many staffers and managers and too few leaders. Our educational system turns out MBAs who learn how to do but not how to envision and lead. Look at most MBA curricula—you will not see the entrepreneurial skills needed to lead.

Within the problem-solving domain, we must develop problem-finding teams. Their job is to detect problems before they become crises, and to seek out improvement projects that will move an organization forward.

Effective problem solving begins with deciding whether to

form a team or attack the problem alone, selecting the team members, writing an effective charter, and reorienting our teams to be more proactive.

WHY FORM HETEROGENEOUS GROUPS?

Critical thinking is more important than team tranquility. And the quest for critical thinking begins with having the right mix of team members. Avoid selecting team members who are clones of one another. Remember, similar members think alike. They reinforce each other's opinions and mistake unanimity of opinion for a thorough analysis.

Form heterogeneous groups. Include people with different skills, roles, and viewpoints. This is the key to fostering a critical-thinking attitude within the group. More specifically, heterogeneous groups can accomplish the following five goals:

1. Reality-test ideas and assumptions.
2. Improve the odds of a successful implementation.
3. Co-opt hostile opposition to group ideas.
4. Perform the multiple roles that are necessary for an effective group effort.
5. Create and resolve doubt during the problem-solving process.

Reality-test Ideas

Groups often have no way of knowing whether their ideas are valid. This happens because members who are similar think alike too. Thus, they mistake agreement for truth. The lack of controversy may be desired in social clubs; in problem-solving teams, however, it is the kiss of death. When members are alike, they may find it difficult to subject their ideas to rigorous analysis or scrutiny.

Getting Solutions Implemented

Often problem-solving teams must implement their solutions. If this requires judgment and creativity, the installers must be committed to the solution. Judgment and creativity are needed when the path to implementation is strewn with obstacles and landmines. When decisions involve the realignment of power or resources within a department or firm, their implementation will be difficult and calls for the highest levels of commitment. If the implementation is cut-and-dried, then commitment is not needed.

How can you achieve the needed level of commitment? Have the installers join the problem-solving team. This way they may feel ownership in the decision and work harder to make it succeed.

Overcome Opposition

When decisions are controversial, someone's ox will be gored. For the sake of harmony, do you exclude those who are likely to be opposed to your initial thoughts and plans? Or, do you involve them as team members and listen to what they have to say? Both options can cause problems. However, the more risky option is to exclude those whose positions differ from the beliefs and views of the majority. If you exclude them, team meetings will be more tranquil. But it is only a temporary lull before the storm. After announcing your decision, the "excluded ones" will seek to ambush your solution. While including minority opinion members will raise the heat index in the meetings, they also serve two useful roles. First, you can factor their positions and beliefs into the final decision. Compromise is an acceptable strategy for resolving intragroup conflicts. More important, you may be able to overcome their opposition and gain their support in installing the solution. Remember, the problem-solving game is not over until you have installed the decision and corrected the problem.

Where do you want your aggravation? During the decision-making process where you can honestly respond to others' concerns, or after you have made the decision when you may feel the need to defend it? I recommend the former strategy. As the TV commercial that extols the virtues of changing your car's oil filter on a regular basis states, "You can pay me now or you can pay me later."

Multiple Problem-solving Roles

Effective teams require members who can play multiple roles. Some are *explorers*, or entrepreneurs, in search of new ideas or projects to improve departmental performance. Once they identify promising areas, other team members must be *artists*, *scientists*, or *designers*. In these roles, they turn fuzzy ideas into concrete alternatives. Yet others are *judges* who evaluate the merits of the alternative solutions. *Facilitators* maintain a constructive conflict ambience within the group. Too little conflict may lead to groupthink and its attendant problems; too much conflict can lead to chaos and team disintegration. Finally, some team members must be *warriors* who install the alternative solution.

No one person is best at all these roles. Heterogeneous groups are more likely to meet your needs. Homogeneous groups tend to overstock on some roles and ignore others. Supply may not equal demand.

Doubt Creation and Resolution

Creating and resolving doubt is a key to solving ill-structured problems. Premature agreement often leads to solving the wrong problem. When all members are similar, they tend to view problems from only one perspective, thus increasing the chances of selective perception (Chapter 2). Heterogeneous teams tend to generate multiple views of the same problem. This creates doubt. During the group's deliberations, each side has an opportunity to explain and sell its view. Through either compromise or collaboration, the team may develop a high-quality solution.

Earlier I recounted how engineers and psychologists viewed the same problem differently when tenants in a high-rise building complained about slow elevator service. The engineers developed technical solutions such as installing faster elevators or staggering office hours. The psychologists suggested installing mirrors on each floor.

The differences in viewpoints are clear. The engineers saw the problem as technological—slow elevators or high peak demand. The psychologists saw the real problem as involving people. When we have nothing to do, even a one-minute wait seems interminable.

The differences in viewpoints are important. A team of engineers and psychologists would have to explore the assumptions underlying their ideas. How long is a "long" wait? What is the real problem—elevators or people? In short, the team would avoid one of the cardinal sins of groupthink—reaching a premature consensus. In solving ill-structured problems, you must create, manage, and resolve doubt.

THREE STRATEGIES FOR FORMING HETEROGENEOUS GROUPS

INCLUDE INSTALLERS	CREATIVE/DIVERGENT
MULTIPLE STAKEHOLDERS	CREATIVE/DIVERGENT
DECISION STYLE MIX	CREATIVE/DIVERGENT

Include Installers

When installers have helped to forge a decision, they will make the decision work. The installers can be either ex-officio or full-fledged members of the team. The former approach relegates them to second-class citizenship, and may reduce their drive to install *your* (and not their own) solution. Making them full-fledged members increases the size of the problem-solving team and can cause serious group dynamics problems. Communication distortions, conflicts, and status problems increase as the size of a team increases. Whatever the installers' roles, make them a part of your problem-solving team.

Include Multiple Stakeholders

Decisions have an impact on many groups. We need to identify these groups, or *stakeholders*, in a systematic manner. Then we should explicitly consider each group for team membership. Often it is simple to identify stakeholders. If individuals feel strongly about an issue, they will let you know it. At other times, you may not be aware of potential stakeholders. In this case, you will want to consider the following methods for identifying them:

• *Power approach*—Can you think of any individuals or groups who hold power within the organization that might be impacted by your ultimate decision?

• *Fishnet approach*—Who is affected most by a decision? Those closest to it, of course. It is like picking up a fishnet and pulling it taut. While all the knots would be affected, only those closest to the point where the net was pulled taut would move substantially. Look to those groups that are critical to your department's smooth functioning. For example, those departments that either provide inputs to your department or receive your outputs might be most affected by any decision you make.

• *Other-side approach*—Those who are known to be in opposition to either the team's purpose or the positions of known team members.

• *Informal leader approach*—Those who shape the opinions of others in the organization, even if they are not in positions of formal authority.

• *Silent majority approach*—Those who will not or cannot openly confront the group's ultimate decision, but might, nevertheless, undermine it.

Over a decade ago, the Tennessee Valley Authority wanted to construct another dam to generate additional electrical power. They requested input from a variety of groups. Unfortunately, they failed to consult with one important stakeholder—the snaildarter. The dam would destroy the snaildarter's breeding grounds. While the snaildarter could not speak for itself, many environmental groups were not as reticent. As a result, the dam's construction was held up by the courts for many years. The lesson of the story: Consider all important stakeholders for group membership. "Remember the snaildarter!"

Multiple stakeholders are especially appropriate for politically explosive decisions that involve multiple and highly verbal parties. In March 1986, the Metropolitan Atlanta Rapid Transit Authority (MARTA) formed a Committee of 50. The committee's goal was to determine the course of rapid-rail growth in the metro-Atlanta area until the year 2000. The committee's deliberations realistically portray how heterogeneous groups struggle but are often successful in reaching a consensus.

The Committee of 50. In 1968, Fulton and DeKalb counties rejected a rapid-rail transit referendum. Many black voters felt they were being asked to pay for a pet project of the white business community. In fact, no black precinct supported the referendum. Three years later, MARTA tried again, knowing that they had to court the black community. Initially MARTA promised them a busway running from Perry Homes, a black housing project, to downtown Atlanta. MARTA argued that a busway would be faster than a rail line. A black coalition rejected this proposal and, in a marathon session, forced MARTA to agree to a rail line to the Perry Homes area—the Proctor Creek Line. The black coalition publicly endorsed the plan, and subsequently the referendum passed by a few thousand votes in Fulton and DeKalb counties. Two other metro counties, Clayton and Gwinnett, rejected the referendum. The referendum, which increased the sales tax by 1%, established heavy rail construction priorities (Exhibits 4-1 and 4-2). Heavy rail trains can carry up to eight cars and travel at 60 miles per hour. Power comes from an electric rail, and there is an operator on board each train.

With Phase C scheduled for completion by 1990, the chairman of MARTA felt that another look at Atlanta's rapid transit needs was in order. The explosive growth of the northern suburbs, especially around the GA 400 Highway, made the reexamination even more urgent. Although the Committee of 50's charge was more encompassing, we will focus on only two issues. The committee was asked to reexamine the Phase D and E rail line priorities. They were also to determine if heavy rail or some other form of rapid transit should be used. Alternatives included light rail or trolleys powered from overhead wires, automated guideway transit or people movers, and monorails.

The committee included all 17 MARTA board members; members from DeKalb County, Fulton County, and Atlanta; and members appointed by the governor, the lieutenant governor, and the Speaker of the House. The committee included businessmen, politicians, spokespersons for neighborhood associations, ministers, and educators. All parties with a vested interest in the outcome were represented—the committee was truly a multi-stakeholder team.

The MARTA chairman asked the committee to complete its work within 120 days. The committee's report would then have to be approved by the MARTA board and two of the three local governments (Atlanta, Fulton County, and DeKalb County) before the recommendations would be implemented. The committee scheduled 12 sessions and began meeting in mid-March.

Early on, there were newspaper editorials suggesting that the committee not be bound by the original Phase D and E priorities. Committee member Jim Tysinger, who was appointed by the lieutenant governor, felt that rail line priorities were strictly an economic issue—what lines provide the best service to the greatest number of people at the lowest cost?[4] In one editorial, a columnist noted that convenience was the key issue. How far do you have to walk to reach transportation and how long does it take to get to your required destination?[5] Neither gentleman was totally correct—much of the final compromise involved symbolic issues, and fact and perception were weighted equally.

By early April the committee agreed to change the proposed North Atlanta

EXHIBIT 4-1
Map of MARTA Rapid Transit System

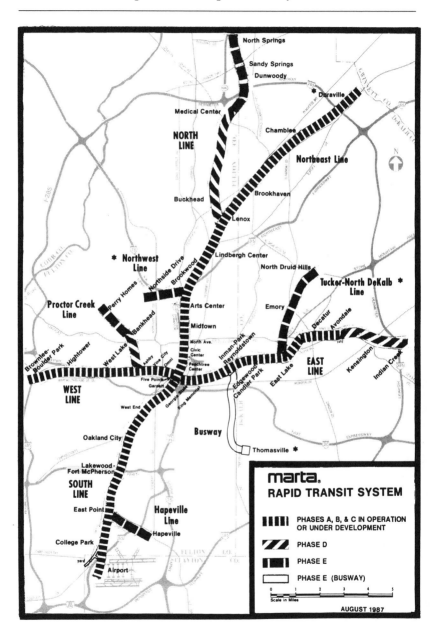

EXHIBIT 4-2
Priorities for Rail Line Construction

Phase A	East-West Line from Avondale to Hightower. North-South Line from North Avenue to Garnett.
Phase B	North-South Line extensions from North Avenue to Brookhaven and from Garnett to Lakewood.
Phase C	North-South Line extensions from Brookhaven to Doraville and from Lakewood to the airport.
Phase D	East-West Line extensions from Avondale to Indian Creek and from Hightower to Brownlee. Proctor Creek Line from the Ashby Station on the West Line to Perry Homes.
Phase E	Hapeville Line, Tucker-North Dekalb Line, and the Northwest Line. Busway from Lenox Station toward GA 400—the North Atlanta Busway.

busway to a rapid rail line. During the 15 years since the original plan, Atlanta's northside had experienced explosive growth. A busway would no longer serve the transportation needs of the primarily white northern suburbs. The committee approved the building of a rapid rail line through the GA 400 highway corridor. The committee did not address the issue of priority or type of rail construction. The committee also avoided taking a position on the hotly contested extension of the GA 400 Highway to Interstate 85, which was then under consideration by the Atlanta City Council. Opposing sides were real estate and business interests, who favored the extension, and suburban homeowners, who opposed building a six-lane highway through their neighborhoods.

The Committee of 50 meeting at which the GA 400 rail line was approved was marked by angry debate and a motion to postpone. Some members felt that the North Atlanta Line would be given precedence over the Proctor Creek Line to the predominantly black Perry Homes community. Nevertheless, the vote was unanimous. That day, David Chesnut, chairman of the Committee of 50, noted that "when it comes time to pick which one to do first, there's going to be a bloodbath."[6] He would not rule out the possibility of a minority report.

In mid-April the committee began to informally talk about substituting an express busway for the Proctor Creek Line. The battle lines were drawn when Mary Sanford, president of the Perry Homes Tenants Association, said, "I want a rail line to go to Proctor Creek, not a busway."[7] It appeared that the group would splinter on the rail line construction priority issue.

The committee began to be subjected to extensive outside lobbying pressures. A subcommittee of the Atlanta City Council tabled a motion to approve the rapid rail line in the GA 400 highway corridor. They wanted to exert pressure on the Committee of 50 to reaffirm top priority to the Proctor Creek Line. A week later, the full Atlanta City Council approved the GA 400 rail line. However, they also passed a nonbinding resolution calling for the construction of the Proctor Creek Line. Others joined in the battle. On 19 June the DeKalb County commissioners passed a resolution stating that the East Rail Line Extensions should either be constructed first or "as first" as the North Atlanta Line. They argued that DeKalb County provided 40% of the operating revenues, while it received only 21% of construction revenues. Mayor Andrew Young of Atlanta also asked for an independent audit of MARTA's cost figures. He argued that if light rail were used (rather than heavy rail), both the Proctor Creek and North Atlanta lines could be built in spite of reduced Federal funding. The manufacturers of the alternative transit systems also questioned MARTA's figures, which showed that heavy rail line was still the least expensive option for the North Atlanta Line.

In June, MARTA released a report that caused an uproar within the committee. It noted that the transit authority could save $50 million by building an express busway from Perry Homes to downtown Atlanta. It would shave ten minutes off the present trip. The report noted that while a heavy rail branch line would cost $123 million, it would save only four minutes. It also provided the following cost estimates for building the North Atlanta Line:

Mode	Cost per mile
Heavy rail	$44.7M per mile
Light rail	$50.2M per mile
Automated guideway transit	$54.9M per mile
Monorail	$50.9M per mile

In another report, MARTA estimated that there would be 13,400 riders per hour on the North Atlanta Line, 11,900 riders per hour on the East Line Extension, and only 1,100 riders per hour on the proposed Proctor Creek Line.

With mounting external pressures and MARTA's study reports, the meetings began to heat up. In June, the committee failed to give priority to constructing the Proctor Creek Line. Some black neighborhood advocates thought that they were mere figureheads and that MARTA would do "what it well pleased."[8] However, the committee did pass a resolution that recognized MARTA's "moral obligation" to give the Proctor Creek Line equal consideration with other rail line priorities. The Proctor Creek advocates were not satisfied. They were even more disturbed when Hugh Jordan, MARTA board member from Dekalb County, agreed that MARTA had a moral obligation to build the Proctor Creek Line, but asked, "Must it be first?"[9]

The external pressures continued to mount during the summer. City of Hapeville officials lobbied for their planned rail line (see Phase E). The MARTA chairman noted that an express busway service to Perry Homes was enough of a compromise. He argued that the need for heavy rail service was simply not there. In fact, the Perry Homes population had dropped from 6,666 in 1970 to 3,821 in 1980. The Atlanta Regional Commission projected a continued drop in population, which indicated that a heavy rail line for Proctor Creek could not be justified. Finally, in August, an independent audit team found MARTA's cost estimates "honest and reasonable."[10]

In late July, the committee voted in favor of heavy rail lines for the East-West rail line extensions (see Phase D in Exhibit 4-2). A subcommittee was appointed to study rapid transit alternatives for the North Atlanta Line, and eventually recommended a heavy rail branch line for this route. Although there had been rumors for some time, MARTA now officially recommended an express busway from Perry Homes to downtown Atlanta. This immediately caused a major crisis. "They are trying to renege on their promise," said Mary Sanford, the Perry Homes representative, and she threatened to boycott the proposed express busway.[11] Again the Perry Homes advocates attempted to make construction of the Proctor Creek Line concurrent with any other rail construction. When the motion was tabled, black members walked out of the meeting.

The walkout could have shattered the committee, but it did not. Committee members continued to search for an acceptable compromise with the black representatives. At the committee's last scheduled meeting, it voted to build a *feeder line* for Proctor Creek using some form of light rail or automated guideway transit. This was a compromise between the more expensive heavy rail branch and the less expensive express bus line. Unlike a *branch line*, a feeder line requires riders to transfer to the heavy rail line to reach downtown. While this approach is much slower than both the heavy rail branch line and the express bus line, neighborhood groups accepted it. As Mary Sanford said, "We need something to appease the community."[12]

The committee's final recommendations were to build:

1. A heavy rail extension on the East-West Line. In the first phase (six to nine years) they recommended the construction of the East Line extension to Indian Creek. In phase two, the West Line would be extended to the Brownlee Station.
2. A rail system from the Ashby Street Station to Perry Homes. In the first phase they recommended construction to the Bankhead Station. In phase two this line would be extended from Bankhead to Perry Homes.
3. A branch line in the North Atlanta corridor. In the first phase they recommended construction from the North Line to the Medical Center Station. In phase two this line would be extended from the Medical Center to North Springs.
4. The city of Hapeville Line would be constructed during phase two.
5. The long-range plan (beyond the year 2010) included the balance of the original referendum system.

What the Committee of 50 understood was that sometimes perceptions are as important as facts. Issues transcend economics. While slower and less convenient to the Perry Homes Community, a feeder line was seen as a high-status transportation symbol. With a rail line for the predominantly white North Atlanta suburbs, Perry Homes residents did not want to be treated as second-class citizens. Furthermore, the black community insisted that MARTA keep its pledge for rail service made in 1971.

A compromise was possible because all stakeholders were represented on the committee. Even though the meetings were heated, the representative parties were able to resolve their differences and reach a consensus. Only when conflicting sides talk to one another is compromise possible. To exclude critical stakeholders from your team is to settle for temporary harmony rather than true consensus.

Include Members with Different Decision Styles

We must create and resolve doubt within the group. One way of doing this is to select members from different functional areas. Our view of a problem is often colored by our educational and business training. As we have noted, an engineer and a psychologist are likely to have different perspectives on the same problem. Thus, if you form a crossfunctional problem-solving team, you are likely to generate multiple perspectives. In theory, this should be an effective strategy. Unfortunately, however, it may not be practical. Minority team members may be treated as second-class citizens. The lone accountant in a group of engineers may be the "odd man out." Furthermore, as you import outsiders, you increase security problems. Then, if crossfunctional teams are often impractical, how can we generate multiple perspectives on a problem?

All engineers (or accountants or financial analysts) are not alike. Even though they receive similar training, there are always individual differences. All engineers do not collect, process, and evaluate information in the same way. They differ along Jung's psychological functions of sensing, intuition, thinking, and feeling (Chapter 3). Thus, one strategy for forming heterogeneous teams is to select team members who differ along the four psychological functions.

Remember, in solving a problem all four psychological functions are necessary. The sensing person seeks out the facts of the problem. The intuitor attempts to find relationships or patterns that help explain problem causality. The thinker weighs the pros and cons of each alternative and selects the best one. And finally, the feeler determines the impact of the decision on people and then "fine tunes" the solution. No one person has all these necessary skills. But a team that includes members with all four psychological functions does (Exhibit 4-3). Each psychological function has a unique contribution to make to your team.

Is it even possible to form teams with all four psychological functions represented? Of 986 engineers listed in the Center

EXHIBIT 4-3
Contributions of the Four Psychological Functions

Sensor as Designer	*Intuitor as Explorer or Artist*
Brings up pertinent facts during diagnosis.	Sees the possibilities in alternative generation. Goes beyond what we have done in the past.
Notices what needs to be done.	Deals with ill-structured problems effectively.
Keeps track of details during diagnosis or implementation.	Provides creative insight into problems or alternative solutions.
Seeks hard data to understand the problem.	Finds patterns or relationships in problem symptoms and generates insights.
Can play the devil's advocate role.	Finds problems before they become crises.

Thinker as Judge	*Feeler as Facilitator*
Analyzes the problem.	Is good at persuading others.
Organizes the problem-solving effort.	Can find common ground between different viewpoints.
Critically evaluates the alternatives.	Arouses enthusiasm and sells alternatives or action plans.
Is resolute in the face of opposition.	Helps the group members to communicate with one another.
Seeks supporting data for alternatives.	Helps the group to incorporate personal values and feelings into the decision process.

for Applied Psychological Type Data Base, 53% are Sensors, and 47% are Intuitors, 64% are Thinkers, and 36% are Feelers. Of 402 psychologists, 15% are Sensors, and 44.5% are Thinkers.[13] It is true that different occupations tend to attract different types of people. Nevertheless, you should be able to form heterogeneous groups within a single department.

One behavioral study suggested an alternative way to form heterogeneous groups.[14] Combining the sensing and intuition dimension with the thinking and feeling dimension, they proposed four *managerial styles*—ST(realist), SF(facilitator), NT(inventor), and NF(enthusiast) managers. Thus, a second strategy for forming heterogenous groups is to select team members who have different managerial styles (Exhibit 4-4).

It is possible to form heterogeneous managerial style teams. My multifirm data base of over 1,000 managers contains 41% ST managers, 35% NT managers, 15% SF managers, and 9% NF managers. However, within a single firm, there is somewhat less heterogeneity. Like the individuals who work for them, organizations have unique managerial styles. ST and NT managers tend to predominate in technological-based firms, while SF

EXHIBIT 4-4
Differences in Four Managerial Styles

STs or Realists	*NTs or Inventors*
Focus on facts.	See possibilities.
Use impersonal analysis.	Use impersonal analysis.
Are practical.	Are most concerned with developing new projects in technical or administrative areas.
Are most concerned with solving technical problems.	

SFs or Facilitators	*NFs or Enthusiasts*
Focus on facts.	See possibilities.
Are sociable.	Are people-oriented.
Are most concerned with solving people problems.	Are most concerned with new projects, especially the people side of them.

and NF managers tend to predominate in social service organizations. Thus, it may not be possible within a single department to find all four managerial styles. Even having two different managerial styles on your team, however, should improve your problem-solving performance.

"Darwinian selection" may make it even more difficult to obtain the desired heterogeneity within a team. A study of school administrators revealed that both principals and vice-principals had similar styles to one another, similar styles to the superintendents, and different managerial styles from most teachers.[15] Perhaps superintendents favored, and thus promoted, those teachers who were "in their own image." In that study two styles accounted for 90% of school administrators. But even here it would have been possible to form heterogeneous groups with at least two of the four styles represented.

The third strategy for forming heterogeneous groups is to use Jung's eight *decision-making styles*. Because Introverted Sensing-Dominant and Extroverted Thinking-Dominant managers are over-represented (Exhibit 4-5), you may not find all eight decision-making styles within a department or firm. Nevertheless, you should be able to form heterogeneous teams with several styles represented.

Maximize the variation in psychological function, managerial style, or decision-making style within your team. When teams have eight or more members, consider subdividing the team into several smaller homogeneous subgroups. Each subgroup can tackle a part of the problem (the serial approach to problem solving), or can simultaneously work on the whole problem (the parallel approach). In the parallel approach, the subgroups work independently of one another. On a periodic basis, all the subgroups meet in a *plenary session* to compare notes and reach a consensus action plan. This subdivision strategy also improves communications within each subgroup and provides the opportunity for all to speak.

To summarize:

• For teams with less than eight members, select members so as to *maximize* their differences along the four psychological functions, the four managerial styles, or the eight decision-making styles.

- For teams of eight or more members, form two or more subgroups. Select members and assign them so as to *minimize* the differences within subgroups and *maximize* the differences between subgroups.

EXHIBIT 4-5
Frequency of Eight Decision-making Styles

	Number	*Percentage*
Extrovert with Sensing Dominant	55	5.4%
Introvert with Sensing Dominant	254	24.9
Extrovert with Intuition Dominant	111	10.9
Introvert with Intuition Dominant	131	12.8
Extrovert with Thinking Dominant	247	24.1
Introvert with Thinking Dominant	104	10.1
Extrovert with Feeling Dominant	62	6.0
Introvert with Feeling Dominant	58	5.8
Totals	1,022	100%

Differences within a group can help reality-test ideas, improve implementation odds, co-opt opposition, perform the needed multiple roles, and create and resolve doubt. However, differences can also garble communication among team members, lead to misunderstandings, and produce irreconcilable problems. These problems must be understood and overcome in order to achieve the synergy that heterogeneous groups promise.

Communication Differences. Extroverts and introverts operate differently within groups. Extroverts tend to dominate group meetings, whereas introverts prefer to sit back and reflect on the issues.[16] Introverts may find it difficult to participate in meetings unless the group leader coaxes them into the mainstream. Even within the Nominal Group Technique, introverted team members may choose to be silent during the open discussion period. Under extreme stress conditions, differences are magnified. Extroverts want to affiliate with other team members as a way of coping with the situation; introverts do not.[17]

Sensors and Intuitors "make their case" differently.[18] When presenting or explaining an idea or influencing others, Sensors are factual, work out the details in advance, document previously successful applications, show why the idea makes sense, and try to reduce the risk factors. Intuitors point out future benefits, become enthusiastic and excited, indicate future challenges and opportunities, and provide the "big picture."

Thinkers and Feelers also communicate differently.[19] Thinkers are logical, state the principle behind their reasoning, are well-organized, move logically from point to point, and list cost and benefits. Feelers are friendly, inject moral or ethical issues, and sell ideas by noting who endorses them. If each member fails to recognize and appreciate what others, who are different, bring to the problem-solving effort, synergy is not possible.

The following scenario portrays the potential communication problems within heterogeneous groups.[20]

In an office:

SF manager   Because I am a sensing type, I like detail. But when Carol (an NT) sends me a memo, it is so short that I can never figure out what she is really trying to say. Her memos are so ambiguous. Then she tells me that mine are too long. Hah! At least I give her all the information.

NT manager   Yes, your memos are too long—they go on and on. And another thing Don (SF), sometimes I get an idea and I want to act on it. I know it's good. But you want to know all the details, all the ramifications, and all the statistics. By the time we go through everything, my inspiration is gone.

Somewhat later:

NF manager   You know, I really try to relate to my people, to understand where they are coming from. But when we work on a project with John (ST), he is so curt and businesslike, he forgets about people's feelings. Honestly, I think he is so interested in completing the project that he demotivates my people.

ST manager   That's not true. It's just that I think you spend too much time on communication and not enough time getting the job done. Most of the time I have to keep reminding you what we're here for.

Very much earlier:

> And the Earth had the same language and the same words. . . . Let us, then, go down and confound their speech, so that they shall not understand one another's speech . . . That is why it is called Babel.
>
> —*Genesis* 11:1–8

Our managers do not appear to speak the same language. They mistake individuality for inferiority. What each is saying is, "Why can't you be more like me?" That is not possible; we are what we are. We must appreciate what different managerial or decision-making styles have to offer. An NF manager augments an ST manager. Each compensates for each other's blind spots— if only they can learn to work with one another.

Decision-making style also affects who talks to whom. A team was assembled to concentrate on special projects involving high-energy optical transfer systems.[21] It comprised two mechanical engineers, two optical physicists, a computer scientist, an electrical engineer, and an aeronautical engineer. Several informal subgroups, or cliques, formed. What is interesting is how they formed. Rather than along the lines of functional disciplines, the cliques were based on decision-making style as shown in Exhibit 4-6.

Within a clique, members worked well together and discussed issues and problems. There was much less communication between cliques. The Introverted Sensing-dominant engineers (**IS**Ts) hardly spoke to any other subgroup. The Extroverted Feeling-dominant scientist (**ESF**) spoke only to one other subgroup. Had the leader not intervened and helped the entire group work out its communication problems, the project would have failed.

Conflict-handling Differences. There are several ways to handle conflict within a group. Briefly, *competition* occurs when members

EXHIBIT 4-6
Clique Formation Within a Scientific Team

INTs	ISTs
Optical physicist	Aeronautical engineer
Computer scientist	Mechanical engineer

ESF	INTs
Optical physicist	Mechanical engineer
	Electrical engineer

are assertive about their own positions but are unconcerned with other members' feelings or beliefs. *Collaboration* confronts disagreements openly to find solutions. Here members listen to what others have to say. They understand that differences of opinion force members to support their own beliefs. *Avoidance* causes physical or psychological withdrawal from the group. *Accommodation* seeks group harmony by smoothing over differences between group members. Harmony becomes the master over critical inquiry. *Compromise* seeks a middle ground between opposing positions—if you give, I will give, and we can reach agreement.

Managers with different psychological orientations handle conflict differently.[22] Extroverts use collaboration, while Introverts prefer avoidance. Thinkers often use competition, while Feelers often use accommodation. Sensors and Intuitors use similar strategies. Again we see the need for common ground. How can we get a group of different types to agree on one or several ways to handle the inevitable conflicts that arise within a group? As we will see later on, we must develop a charter.

Decision-making Differences. How managers attack a problem may be related to their decision-making or managerial style. John Slocum asked 152 organizational development specialists what information and tools they used in making an organizational diagnosis of a client's problem.[23] ST specialists most frequently sought task information—information on work processes, job content, and the physical setting. SF and NF specialists most frequently sought people-oriented information—information on informal work groupings, leadership, interpersonal satisfaction, and organizational climate. NT specialists most frequently requested structure information—information on organizational hierarchies, the control and reward system, and resource limitations.

These strategic differences extended to their intervention tactics. STs most often used behavior modification but never used transactional analysis. SFs frequently used transactional analysis but never used behavior modification. NTs most often used survey feedback techniques, and NFs preferred confrontation meetings.

Different approaches to attacking a problem can be effective. Different methods are likely to create doubt. The key issue is, will the group be able to resolve it? If team members quarrel with each other's approaches, much heat and very little light will be shed on the problem. Writing a group charter may cool the group down.

To this point we have discussed three different strategies for forming heterogeneous groups. We have also discussed how heterogeneous groups can accomplish five different problem-solving goals (see Exhibit 4-7 for a summary of these strategies and goals.)

EXHIBIT 4-7
Strategies and Goals of Heterogeneous Groups

STRATEGIES	GOALS				
	Reality Test Ideas	Aid the Implementation	Co-opt Opposition	Multiple Roles	Create and Resolve Doubt
Include implementors	X	X		X	
Include multiple stakeholders	X	X	X		X
Include multiple decision styles	X			X	X

CONSTRUCTING A GROUP CHARTER

How many times have you heard a team leader say, "I think we all know why we are here, so let's get started"? Even though many team leaders are more informative, team members are often confused on the details. And that is unacceptable, because a long-standing team cannot operate effectively without a group charter. Without one they will be as efficient as day laborers at the Tower of Babel. A charter should contain a written understanding of the group's task, its own position within the organization, and its operating rules.

Understanding the Task

What is a team supposed to do? Susan, a senior manager, forms a group to *investigate* a serious drop in morale. She shares with the group her thoughts as to why morale has dropped and what should be done about it. She then asks the group for help. What latitude does the team have? What does the word investigate mean? Does the team have the authority to redefine Susan's assessment? Or must the team accept the problem statement at face value? What if the team determines that falling morale is not the real problem? Suppose it is merely a symptom of a more serious problem. Without an explicit charter, the term "investigate" is ambiguous. Remember, English is not a precise language.

What freedom does the team have to develop solutions? Can they only propose solutions, or will they be involved in the installation? And if they are not involved in the installation, who will be? Is the group a decision-making or an advisory body? Do team members have access to outsiders who can provide information or special knowledge, or must they operate in isolation? The team must also agree on the form that the final report will take as well as its completion date.

Relating to the Organization

What are the team's power bases and resources? In completing a task, a team may be granted formal authority or it may have to rely on somewhat more tenuous power bases, such as expertise or charm. The former works, because knowledge is power. The latter works, because often people will respond to a sincere request. The type of power base often depends on where and how the team fits into the overall organization. Who does it report to? More important, who can the team members turn to if they run into problems with obtaining data, resources, or help from others? In short, who are their "fixers," and what is their motivation to act in this capacity?

As a team member your job is to raise questions that clarify these issues. As team leader, your job is to get answers for your team and to act as a liaison to higher authorities. Perhaps your greatest challenge is to keep the group from getting ahead of itself; that is, jumping ahead to other problem-solving phases before it has written a charter. We know that American managers like action and often proceed without laying the necessary groundwork. However, if you do not know where you are going, any road will take you there.

Agreeing on the Rules

The team should also clearly specify its operating rules. Will it use the Nominal Group Technique? How will it create and resolve doubt during problem diagnosis and alternative generation? How will it handle conflict? Will a "second look" meeting be called after the team has selected the best alternative? In short, a charter describes what is expected of each member and the leader. It is an *explicit* contract between team members. Consider incorporating the following oath into your charter:

> I know that I cannot solve this problem alone. If I could, I would. I will speak up. I will present my ideas clearly, and I will listen to what others have to say. While conflict is not bad, I have no right to attack personally other members. I will defend my own point of view, but if I am wrong, I am willing to modify or change my position. I am not dogmatic. And I will not waste your time.

NORM FORMATION AND CHARTER CONSTRUCTION

A charter is only a piece of paper unless group members "internalize" it. They must make it their own. A charter helps create group norms—the formal or informal rules that teams adopt to regulate and regularize important behaviors.[24] Norms develop only for those behaviors that ensure group success, help members learn what is and is not permissible, reinforce individual roles within the group, or express the central values of the group. While norms develop slowly, they often have a powerful and consistent influence on members' behavior.

A team is experiencing difficulty in completing its task. A member suggests that the team should review its progress up to that point. The unplanned review identifies the bottlenecks that have caused the group to fall behind schedule. Several weeks later, a team member suggests it might be time for another review. Again the progress review is helpful. Over time, the group elevates the review process to norm status, for it believes the review helps ensure team success. And the norm will be enforced. Any team member will feel free to demand a review when the group falls behind schedule again.

Groups develop norms that express their central values. One college dean I know closes the door to his conference room one minute after he starts a meeting. What he is saying is that if you cannot be on time, don't come. Promptness has become an important group norm and is never violated.

Norms also define acceptable behaviors. Do presenters really want feedback on their presentations? What is an acceptable level and form of disagreement with the team leader or senior members? How much podium time do junior people really get? Norms increase predictability and reduce uncertainty. In short, norms define a team's culture.

Finally, norms reinforce individual members' roles. Who will keep track of details? Who will break the tension if the meeting gets hot? Whose job is it to find out what is happening in other parts of the organization that might affect the team's chances of success? Who will play the artist's role, the judge's role, or the warrior's role? The norms help identify the role players.

Writing a charter is an explicit attempt to orchestrate norm formation. If, over time, group members internalize the charter, its provisions will become norms. However, unless the charter provisions are actually implemented and reinforced, they will become worthless. Suppose a group's charter proclaims that everyone is free to critique the team leader. If the first time this happens the leader puts that person down, everyone knows what behaviors are desired or tolerated. A charter can provide a set of operational guidelines for the group. Use it or lose it.

All team members are actively involved in developing norms when they are part of a charter. When norms develop from casual statements, critical events, primacy, or carryover behaviors, the leader or senior members play a more significant role.

Casual Statements

When a team leader or senior person speaks, everyone listens. After his first meeting, John, a senior team member, takes Bill, his protégé, aside and tells him in a fatherly way, "The way to get ahead in this firm is to find ways to agree with your superiors." Bill follows John's advice and is rewarded by the team leader. Other junior members see what is happening and adopt the same strategy. What started out as merely friendly advice has now become a group norm, which controls and regulates group behavior. If left unchecked, the norm can blossom into groupthink.

Casual statements need not be negative; nor are the resulting norms counterproductive. However, unless successfully challenged, casual statements can take on an importance far beyond their intended impact.

Critical Events

Critical events establish important precedents and may ultimately develop into norms. During the Cuban missile crisis, Arthur Schlesinger had serious reservations about the Bay of Pigs invasion. The Attorney General told Schlesinger in the strongest terms "not to push it any further." Such critical events led group members to develop a norm of withholding doubts from the President.[25]

Critical incidents can also help formulate productive norms. After a particularly successful meeting, several team members might say, "I think the reason we got so much done was that we started at 7:00 A.M." Others might agree, and an early meeting norm begins to develop. Once it is established, those who are late will be "punished." If their tardiness continues, the latecomers will be psychologically removed from the group. That is, other group members may exclude them from group discussions, devalue their opinions, give them less podium time, or drive them from the group.

Primacy

In the absence of a charter, early group behaviors are perpetuated. Members expect them to continue, and over time, the behaviors become normative. This often happens in classrooms. A student randomly selects a seat for the first class and will probably continue to sit in that seat for the entire quarter. This behavior eliminates the need to "decide" where to sit. Primacy works on the principle that "if it ain't broke, don't fix it."

Suppose that at a team's first meeting, the leader presents a problem and immediately suggests its causes. If this happens at the next few meetings, the members may expect the leader to always make an opening presentation. This is not necessarily the plan or even the desire of the group. The team could remove the norm by challenging the leader's right to always make an initial presentation.

Carryover Behaviors

Very few of us are first-time team members. We tend to carry over successful behaviors from previous groups or work experiences. As students, we did this all the time. Every class was different, yet as students our roles varied little from class to class. Whatever we did to survive in one quarter, we continued to do in the next. Occasionally this strategy backfires. It happens to teams as well.

When team members bring vastly different team experiences to a new group, confusion and uncertainty occurs. Each member has a different understanding of what constitutes acceptable behavior. The confusion is exacerbated when a new team leader or senior team member joins the group. Their ways of doing things may be different from the prevailing norms, and it may take time and effort to "renorm" the group. This can be minimized if the group writes an explicit charter. A charter allows group members to confront and resolve their differences openly.

When norms evolve from casual statements, critical events, primacy, and carry-over behaviors, the courtship period is extended, and it takes longer for the group to work effectively.

The difficulty of re-norming a group is best illustrated by the appointment of Warren Burger as Chief Justice of the Supreme Court in 1969. The norms under the Warren Court failed, and much time and effort were wasted in developing new norms. The old norms that had worked so effectively were, in part, to blame for delays in developing new norms.

When Old Norms Fail—The Evolution of the Burger Court.
Members of the Warren Court evolved a series of unspoken *procedural norms* that helped them focus and resolve legal differences of opinion. After reviewing a case, they would meet and take a preliminary vote. The most senior justice in the majority then assigned a majority member to write a first draft of the opinion. If the chief justice were in the majority, he assigned the case since he is considered the most senior justice. Thus, through this assignment process a justice wielded power. He could assign the opinion to a colleague who wrote narrow opinions or to one who preferred broader interpretations that could produce significant ramifications beyond the particulars of the case. The draft writer would then circulate the opinion for consideration. However, the justices hardly ever met face-to-face to resolve differences. They used their legal clerks, wrote memos suggesting "minor changes" (often of a significant nature), or made notes on the original draft.[26]

Over time, these behaviors evolved into a "norm of indirect persuasion." It permitted justices to engage in substantive legal conflicts without formally admitting that their positions differed greatly. The opinion writer could also make face-saving changes without appearing to submit to his colleagues. Face-to-face confrontation or coalition formation were avoided, for this might be interpreted as lobbying for one's own viewpoint. As the norm worked well during the Warren Court, the justices continued this practice when Warren Burger was appointed chief justice. The norm then proved counterproductive.

Chief Justice Burger made some radical changes in the method of assigning and writing opinions. He increasingly withheld or changed his vote in conference, giving him the power of assignment by continually placing him in the majority.[27] He even assigned a case to a minority member because he did not think there was much difference between the two positions.[28] Occasionally he would write the opinion in order to put a "little something for everyone" into it even though there were widely divergent views.[29] Often Burger failed to recognize or acknowledge major differences between himself and other members of the majority.[30] Finally, he removed the law clerks from the informal network that had previously worked so well. Clearly, Burger was changing the ground rules.

The other justices should have questioned these sweeping procedural changes openly. There were some half-hearted attempts at open confrontation, but these failed to gain wide support. The justices did not wish to lecture the chief justice, nor were they ready to confront him directly.[31] Furthermore, they believed that the carryover norm of indirect persuasion was the proper approach. After all, it had worked in the Warren Court. They refused to address the real problem—the method that Burger used in assigning an opinion. Rather they resorted to behind-the-scenes attempts to change the *legal content* of his drafted opinions.

This subterranean strategy failed for two reasons. First, it did not address the procedural issues problem. Instead, it focused on how to change an opinion once it had been drafted. That did not work because often Burger simply denied or ignored the differences that other justices raised through their memos. The norm of indirect persuasion was apparently too subtle. The irony was that, by focusing on the legal rather than procedural issues, the justices made it very difficult to reach agreement, and opinions were delayed.

Both sides were to blame. Burger avoided or denied that there were substantive differences in legal views between himself and the majority members. The other justices avoided directly confronting the real issue of procedural changes and focused on the substantive legal issues. The more they pushed substantive changes in an opinion, the more the chief justice denied these differences. And the more he denied their recommended changes, the greater the number of changes they suggested. Here was Catch-22 at its worst. The situation was unstable, and new norms had to evolve.

Finally, in 1975 the justices changed their tactics, and decided to face the procedural problems head-on. They *openly* formed coalitions to challenge the *procedural problems*; that is, they challenged Burger's right to assign an opinion. For example, the chief justice assigned Justice Byron White to write a draft opinion in five capital punishment cases. Justices Lewis Powell, Potter Stewart, and John Stevens, all majority members, openly declared their intent to write an alternative opinion. Their opinion would reach the same conclusion but would be based on different legal reasoning. Justice White then submitted the case back to the conference for reassignment. The coalition then forced Burger to reassign the case to one of its members. With this strategy, a new norm regulating the assignment procedure was forged.

The norm of indirect persuasion, while successful in resolving substantive legal issues in the Warren Court, was inadequate to deal with procedural problems in the Burger Court. What the court needed was an "open confrontation" norm. It took almost six years to develop one. Old habits die slowly, even when they are no longer productive.

FINDING PROBLEMS AND OPPORTUNITIES

POUNDS'S MODEL	CREATIVE/DIVERGENT
PROBLEM SCOUTING	CREATIVE/DIVERGENT

A manager's job transcends problem solving. Managers must also find problems. They must seek out potential improvement projects or identify developing problem situations before they become crises. In short, managers must design an early warning system.

What is a problem? It is a performance gap between where we are and (1) where we were, (2) where we expected to be, or (3) where we would like to be. For example, "For the last several quarters we had 5% absenteeism. Now we are experiencing 10%." Why has there been an increase? Performance gaps can also signal improved performance. Suppose we experience a sudden and unexpected drop in absenteeism. If the causes are not determined, we will not be able to maintain the lower levels of absenteeism. Problem finding is gap identification, and problem solving is gap closing.

How do managers find these gaps? From William Pounds's pioneering study, we know that they use mental models to help them define acceptable levels of departmental performance.[32] The models are not explicit, mathematical, or formal. Nevertheless, managers create them in one of the following four ways:

Historic Models

Based on the assumption that the best estimate of the future is the recent past, managers expect continuity of performance. Whatever happened in the recent past should continue into the near future. And if it does not, we have a performance gap. Is our safety record better than last quarter's? Has there been a significant drop in sales from last year? Here it is important to review standard accounting, marketing, or departmental reports generated by the organization's information system.

Planning Models

Planning models provide detailed projections of performance for the upcoming years. When actual performance fails to meet budgeted levels, we may have a potential problem. Unfortunately, budgeted performance levels are often set so low that most managers exceed them. Thus planning models produce few, if any, performance gaps. When planning is based on realistic goals, variances between actual and budgeted performance will reveal latent problems.

Other People's Models

Some models are maintained by other people. Customers who purchase poor quality products from a firm will notify management of their disappointment. Now the manager has a problem. A senior manager's "blue-skying" becomes his or her subordinates' challenge. The organization is a channeling mechanism. It directs problems identified by senior managers to staff members who are especially qualified to solve them.

Extra-organizational Models

Trade journals, competitors, other divisions within the organization, or professional conferences can sometimes define performance gaps. Is there a difference between our performance and our West Coast operations? Should we handle this situation the way our competitors do? Should we adopt a new procedure seen at a trade show? How do we compare to published industry-wide performance levels?

Extenuating factors may explain a gap. For example, the West Coast operation may have new equipment, and our equipment is outdated. But that is problem solving, and our concern here is to identify potential performance gaps—without that, there can be no problem solving.

Extra-organizational models focus on the external environment. Thus, your organization's information system will be of little use here. Rather, your informal network of colleagues throughout the industry or country will provide much of the data in developing your extra-organizational models.

Once managers choose a model, they then use it to evaluate current performance. The manager identifies important differences, selects one for examination, and begins the problem-solving process.

The managers in Pounds's study used four approaches to identify latent problems or opportunities. Teams also play an essential role in an early warning system.

PROBLEM-FINDING TEAMS

Begin by forming a heterogeneous problem-finding team. Then have the group identify potential problems or improvement projects. Team members should assess both internal and external *Weaknesses, Opportunities, Threats,* or *Strengths* (WOTS) in terms of the following: managerial, markets and products, facilities, finance, competition, suppliers, organizational structure, and so forth.[33] Using the Nominal Group Technique, have each member complete a form like the one shown in Exhibit 4-8.

This form is based on the Rational Argumentation Model described in Chapter 2. Each member must provide supporting data for his or her potential problem or improvement project. Here you can use Pounds's four models. Warrants tell others why a particular model is relevant for your claim. The rebuttal

EXHIBIT 4-8
WOTS Problem/Improvement Project Finding Form

| Opportunity | _____ | Strength | _____ |
| Threat | _____ | Weakness | _____ |

Claim: Potential Problem or Improvement Project

Supporting Data:

Warrant:

Rebuttal:

provides an escape valve that tells others under what conditions the model may no longer be valid and, therefore, the claim incorrect. Exhibit 4-9 contains examples of a completed WOTS Problem-Finding Form.

EXHIBIT 4-9
Two Completed WOTS Problem-Finding Forms

Dimension: A potential managerial problem

Claim:	Approximately 25% of the middle managers received a poor performance rating this past year.
Data:	Historical Model—In the previous two years, only 8% of the middle managers received a poor performance rating.
Warrant:	No extenuating circumstances (such as a new CEO or new set of strategic goals) could account for the drop in performance.
Rebuttal:	Could this be an example of statistical regression to the mean?

Dimension: A product or market opportunity

Claim:	Strong growth is forecast for the demand for computers in India.
Data:	Extra-organizational Model—This claim is based on a recently published report by the Worldwide Computer Group.
Warrant:	Worldwide Computer is a highly respected organization and has an excellent track record of predicting future trends in the computer industry.
Rebuttal:	However, I heard on the street that the firm's best forecaster recently left. The India forecast may not be up to their previous standards.

Team members silently and independently generate potential problems and improvement projects. Each presents a list during the round-robin phase. During the open discussion phase, members evaluate each other's ideas. The worthiness of the data, warrants, and rebuttals are used to rank order the potential problem list. If a consensus cannot be reached, the group should use a secret ballot.

Now problem solving can begin. Why has managerial peformance dropped in the last year? Or what can our firm do to exploit a rapidly growing market for computers in India? *Potential problems or improvement projects must be identified before anything can happen.* If you do not know that a problem exists or an opportunity is knocking, you will not take any action. Problem finding may be a critical factor that differentiates successful and less successful firms.

SUMMARY

A critical-thinking attitude does not just happen. You must plant it within the group and nurture it. The process begins with selecting or assigning the right members to the team. Consider including installers and multiple stakeholders. Assign members with differing psychological functions, managerial styles, or decision-making styles. When a team has more than eight members, consider subdividing it into several smaller homogeneous subgroups.

Then help the team write a charter. It should include understanding the task, the team's relationship to the rest of the organization, and how the group will operate. Either you explicitly develop a charter or you passively await the emergence of norms within the group. When norms emerge, only the team leader or the senior members play an important role. In developing a charter, everyone participates. The choice is yours.

Finally, critical thinking is enhanced as teams seek to identify emerging problems and significant improvement projects. Consider using Pounds's model and problem-finding teams. Remember you cannot solve a problem until you know that it is out there.

ENDNOTES

1. Warren Bennis and Burt Nanus, *Leaders* (New York: Harper and Row, 1985), 60.

2. Irving Lane, et al., "Making the Goals of Acceptance and Quality Explicit," *Small Group Behavior* 13, no. 4 (1982): 542–54; Randy

Hirokawa, "A Comparative Analysis of Communication Patterns within Effective and Ineffective Decision Making Groups," *Communication Monographs* 47 (1980): 312–21.

3. Harvey J. Brightman, "The Structure of the Unstructured Merger Decision." (Paper presented at the annual meeting of the Decision Sciences Institute, Las Vegas, Nevada, November 1985.)

4. *DeKalb Neighbor*, 19 March 1986.

5. *Atlanta Journal*, 10 August 1986, Section C.

6. *Atlanta Journal*, 14 April 1986.

7. *Atlanta Journal*, 27 July 1986, Section A.

8. *Atlanta Constitution*, 5 June 1986, Section B.

9. *DeKalb News-Sun*, 18 June 1986.

10. *Atlanta Constitution*, 7 August 1986, Section C.

11. *Atlanta Journal*, 24 July 1986, Section B.

12. *DeKalb News-Sun*, 14 August 1986, Section A.

13. Isabel Briggs Myers and Mary McCaulley, *Manual: A Guide for the Development and Use of the Myers-Briggs Type Indicator* (Palo Alto, California: Consulting Psychologist Press, 1985), 244–52.

14. Ian Mitroff, Vincent Barabba, and Ralph Kilmann, "The Application of Behavioral and Philosophical Technologies to Strategic Planning: A Case Study of a Large Federal Agency," *Management Science* 24, no. 1 (September 1977): 44–58.

15. Harvey J. Brightman, "Improving Principals' Performance Through Training in the Decision Sciences," *Educational Leadership* (February 1984): 30–36.

16. Myers and McCaulley, *Manual*, 131.

17. Ralph Kilmann and Kenneth Thomas, "Interpersonal Conflict Handling as Reflections of Jungian Personality Dimensions," *Psychological Reports* 37 (1975): 971–80.

18. Sandra Krebs Hirsh, *Using the Myers-Briggs Type Indicator in Organizations* (Palo Alto, California: Consulting Psychologist Press, 1985), Reproducible Master #44.

19. Ibid.

20. Dorothy Hai, *What Type of Manager Are You?* (Murray Hill, New Jersey: Bell Laboratories, 1980), 4–7.

21. Robert Doering, "Enlarging Scientific Task Team Creativity," *Personnel* (March-April 1972): 43–52.

22. Kilmann and Thomas, "Interpersonal Conflict Handling," 978.

23. John Slocum, "Does Cognitive Style Affect Diagnosis and Intervention Strategies of Change Agents?" *Group and Organizational Studies* (June 1979): 199–210.

24. Daniel Feldman, "The Development and Enforcement of Group Norms," *Academy of Management Review* 9, no. 1 (1984): 47–53.

25. Irving Janis, *Groupthink: Psychological Studies of Policy Decisions and Fiascos* (New York: Houghton Mifflin, 1982).

26. Bob Woodward and Scott Armstrong, *The Brethren: Inside the Supreme Court* (New York: Simon and Schuster, 1979), 28, 252, 377.

27. Ibid., 170–74.

28. Ibid., 100.

29. Ibid., 196.

30. Ibid., 66.

31. Patricia Palmertona and Paula Pribble, "The Brethren: A Case Study." (Paper presented at the Western Speech Communication Association, Denver, 1982), 10–14.

32. William F. Pounds, "The Process of Problem Finding," *Industrial Management Review* (Fall 1969): 1–19.

33. George Steiner, *Strategic Planning: What Every Manager Must Know* (New York: Free Press, 1979), 142–46.

DIAGNOSIS
and
ALTERNATIVE
GENERATION

In the last chapter you learned to identify performance gaps. Now you will learn to close them. Diagnosis and alternative generation are the most critical problem-solving activities. Here you diagnose the problem, generate skeletal ideas, screen them, and then flesh out the best ones. If you do not know what caused a problem or have not formulated decision goals, you cannot design effective solutions. To paraphrase Shakespeare, "There's small choice in rotten apples or ineffective alternatives." In this chapter you will learn to produce good apples.

PROBLEM CLASSIFICATION

We are familiar with the term "diagnosis" as used in the medical field. The doctor asks questions and runs tests to determine the patient's illness. But what does diagnosis mean in business problems solving? It depends on the type of problem we face.

There are two types of problems—disturbance and entrepreneurial. Both are gaps between "what is" and some goal. However, the goals differ, as the following indicates:

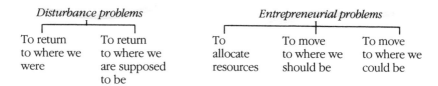

Disturbance problems		*Entrepreneurial problems*		
To return to where we were	To return to where we are supposed to be	To allocate resources	To move to where we should be	To move to where we could be

A disturbance, or crisis, problem is a gap between your previous or budgeted levels of performance and your present performance. Your goal is to eliminate that gap. Here you use Pounds's historic or planning models (Chapter 4) to become aware of the gap.[1] For example, your department experiences a sudden and dramatic decrease in productivity. Alternatively, there has been a jump in absenteeism. The common thread in both examples is that there is a *deviation* from historical or budgeted performance levels.

An entrepreneurial problem, or improvement project, is a gap between your present performance and a higher or desired level of performance. Again your goal is to shrink the gap. In this case, you use either Pounds's other peoples' or extra-organizational models to sense opportunities. For example, one of your competitors has just installed an office automation system. Your superior asks you "to look into it." In effect he is asking, "Should we also purchase a system, and if so, which one?" Alternatively, a senior manager wonders if the firm should offer a new service. Your team might be asked to examine its feasibility. The common thread in both examples is the belief that department performance can be improved.

AN OVERVIEW OF DIAGNOSIS
AND ALTERNATIVE GENERATION

Exhibit 5-1 outlines the recommended practice for analyzing both types of problems.

EXHIBIT 5-1
**Recommended Practice in Diagnosing Problems
and Generating Alternative Solutions**

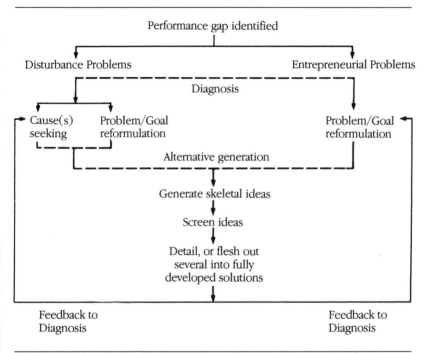

Disturbance Problems

You have identified a gap. If you do not know what caused it, you must determine its cause. If you know its cause(s), then diagnosis means reformulating the problem goals.

First ask yourself: What factor or factors caused the deviation from budgeted or historical levels of performance? Seeking causes is like finding a needle in a haystack. The needle is the problem cause, and for ill-structured problems, the haystack is very large and the needle very small.

You will learn a convergent and logical approach, the Kepner and Tregoe Method, and a divergent and creative approach, the Alternative Worldview Method. The former uses a systematic search strategy to find the elusive needle; the latter generates multiple possible causes in your search for causality. Remember, teams that identify causes outperform those that do not.[2]

When you know the causes but still have not been able to solve the problem, reformulate it. Ask:
- Where do we want to be?
- What is our goal?
- What should our goals be?
- Can we restate or reformulate our goals?

You will also learn two creative techniques for problem reformulation—the 5Ws and Problem Boundary Expansion methods. Each produces radically different alternative solutions, especially when coupled with creative alternative generating techniques.

Your team must then develop alternative solutions. Your diagnosis will affect the alternatives you propose. Consider an organization that has a cash-flow problem. The accounts receivable and accounts payable have become unbalanced. Should you define the problem as how to balance cash flows or as how to increase revenue? A revenue problem definition may cause you to redesign products or services. A cash-flow problem may cause you to conduct a financial analysis to find ways to balance the funds flow. How you define a problem restricts your search for solutions. Diagnosis and alternative generation are two sides of the same coin. Remember, an acceptable solution to the right problem beats the best solution to a wrong problem.

Generate a large number of skeletal ideas. These are broad solution outlines that can be written on a single page. They should include a brief explanation of the idea, a defense, and very rough estimates of the costs and benefits. You will learn two divergent and creative approaches for generating skeletal ideas—the Nominal Group Technique and Analogy.

Now you must reduce your list to a manageable size. I will present two screening methods—the Nominal Group Technique and Ben Franklin's Moral Algebra. Here you determine which skeletal ideas should be fleshed out into fully developed solutions. Your ultimate goal is to develop at least two truly different alternative solutions consistent with the identified causes.

If none of your initial solutions solve the problem, you can either (1) design or seek additional skeletal ideas, (2) reanalyze the causes, or (3) reformulate the problem.

Entrepreneurial Problems

Once you have identified a performance gap, your team must formulate or reformulate the decision goals. For an entrepreneurial problem there are no deviations from expected performance. There are no causes; there are no needles. Rather, the goal is to move toward some new level of performance. Consider the 5Ws or Problem Boundary Expansion methods to develop alternative goal formulations. Then develop numerous skeletal ideas and try to flesh out at least two truly different solutions. If you do not solve the problem, you can either (1) generate more skeletal ideas, or (2) reformulate the goals and then generate additional ideas.

PROBLEMS IN REAL-WORLD PRACTICE

Diagnosing Problems

Managers or teams often skip diagnosis completely.[3] Once a gap is identified, they propose alternative solutions. There is little analysis to improve problem understanding or to set decision goals. A team of organizational researchers led by Henry Mintzberg studied how senior managers diagnose strategic problems.[4] Decisions included acquiring firms, purchasing expensive equipment, and developing new products and services. Can you imagine making these types of decisions without some form of diagnosis? Yet, in 11 of 25 cases, there was no evidence of an explicit diagnosis. Presumably, diagnosis was informal and implicit. Mintzberg suggested that there simply was not enough time to investigate the problems. Under crisis conditions, we are not at our best.[5] Perhaps so, but there are at least two other possible explanations. The senior managers may not have been aware of diagnostic methods. After all, most colleges do not offer courses in problem diagnosis. Moreover, managers like the action world of seeking solutions, not the reflective world of diagnosis.[6]

One other study showed greater evidence of diagnosis. Of 33 strategic problems, in only 2 cases did organizations actually develop solutions without explicitly questioning or gathering information about the problem.[7]

The decisions in the two previous studies were strategic in nature. In some instances they affected the firm's very existence. Yet in almost one-fourth of the problems the firms conducted no formal diagnosis. Is it not more likely that diagnosis is ignored in solving less strategic problems?

Even when we do formal diagnoses, we often jump to conclusions about causes. A worker's performance has dropped. What is the cause? The worker and his supervisor are likely to offer different answers. The worker may initially blame the drop on external factors such as recent task changes. A worker remarks: "I was doing fine until *they* changed my job. Now I don't know what I'm supposed to do." Supervisors whose bonuses are based on their workers' performances often blame their workers.[8] What we have here is the familiar "protect-your-backside" (PYB) strategy—I'm not to blame; the problem is due to others or to factors beyond my control.

When an entire department's performance drops, managers often jump to one of several PYB conclusions. They may blame the drop on external factors over which they have little or no control.[9] Thus, for example, the drop is due to the installation of a new materials requirements planning system. Or managers may blame one or two workers within the group.[10] They float the "few bad apples" argument. Senior management often blames individual workers, not the supervisor.[11] Senior managers usually are unfamiliar with low-level tasks, and therefore assume that the workers must be at fault. Furthermore, senior managers have a broader view of the entire firm. If only one group within a plant is doing poorly, it cannot be the manager for he or she may be managing several groups.

As group failures accumulate, managers may shift from external to internal causes. Coaches do this. In the first year they blame their poor standings on a tough schedule or injuries. After several losing seasons, the coach starts blaming his players for not working hard enough. Ultimately, the coach determines the real cause or is fired, and the cycle begins anew.

Jumping to conclusions is not a formal diagnosis. It may be appropriate as a first step. In fact, we may not be able to stop doing it. But it is not a formal analysis. Identify it for what it is—a diagnostic bias, like the biases presented in Chapter 2. Jumping to conclusions may cause you to solve the wrong problem.

In practice, diagnosis involves social and political factors, some of which have little to do with diagnostic accuracy.[12] For example, a manager's credibility can influence whether or not his view of a problem is accepted. However, even highly credible managers must present hard facts or data to support their views. However, well-supported views are often rejected when presented by less than credible managers. Data still speaks, even if with a muted voice.

A manager's level of commitment affects diagnosis. Commitment expedites diagnosis when managers do their homework, are enthusiastic, and offer many possibilities. Commitment delays diagnosis when much heat but very little light is shed on the problem. As one manager said: "Decisions aren't made on emotional debate. That's not the type of decision maker you want."[13]

Political factors invade diagnosis. Some managers disguise problem symptoms when they threaten their careers. Others will not define a problem if it means "fingering" present senior management. Often people-centered problems are deliberately diagnosed as technical problems. As one manager said, "A human problem is more difficult to formulate than a production problem, which is more readily identifiable."[14] Yet this may lead to solving the wrong problem. Sometimes politics causes important information to be withheld. One manager "twisted slowly in the wind" as he waited for the necessary information to defend his analysis. In short, fear of retaliation, power struggles, and a PYB atmosphere often stifles diagnosis. Apparently, the Marquis of Queensberry rules are not used in the diagnostic arena.

Generating Alternative Solutions

Managers do not generate skeletal ideas, explicitly screen them, and then flesh them out; rather they do all three activities simultaneously. Screening ideas is an implicit part of the search for solutions. Even before managers share ideas with their team members, they are already evaluating them. This leads to self-censorship and is therefore counterproductive.

Studies by decision scientists, Paul Nutt and Henry Mintzerg, suggest that managers generate solutions in three ways.[15] The most common approach is the Timid Explorer Model. The manager uses one of three strategies to search for alternatives:

• First the manager determines how others *within* or *outside* the organization have solved similar problems.

This approach is risk-free and relatively cheap. A "carbon copy" alternative will probably work too, since others have already tried it successfully. This approach is standard practice in the medical field. First, a prestige medical school or hospital adopts an innovative therapy or treatment. Soon other hospitals fall into line. The second-tier hospitals minimize their risk by waiting for the initial adopter to iron out the problems.

• Second, the manager asks vendors or suppliers to suggest solutions.

If you need to improve your visual presentations at board meetings, why not ask your office equipment supplier for help? While they are not in the presentation business, they may know what others are doing. For example, one of your competitors may be using 35-mm slides made from an inexpensive computer package. The vendor gives you a name to contact at the firm, and you are on the way.

- Third, the manager waits for solutions to arrive.

Each day managers receive unsolicited announcements of products or services that will solve all their ills. Occasionally there is a match between these remedies and an unsolved problem. This strategy will not work for crisis problems that must be solved immediately.

All three of these strategies search familiar terrain. Often the solutions are clones of one another and of present practice.[16] Hence the name, the timid explorer. There is not much risk, but there is little chance of developing a truly innovative solution. That is not how Domino's Pizza developed its revolutionary idea of home delivery, or how for-profit hospitals began to market their specialized services. If everyone copies everyone else, how will innovations be developed? In discussing a recent acquisition, a merger team member made a remark that evidenced a follow-the-leader search strategy.[17] He told me that his firm could now consider acquiring wineries because their major competitor had recently purchased one. He believed that his acquisition team would now receive authorization to proceed from senior management.

Managers also use the Pet Solution Model. Problem solving begins with pet solutions. Now managers seek problems that their solutions will solve. And they will not stop until they have implemented their solutions. For example, a CEO had long hoped to compete with several physician-owned, for-profit laboratories in the community. He selectively interpreted environmental trends and carefully orchestrated on-site visits to such labs until everyone was sold on the idea. Now, with everyone convinced of the need, he build the laboratory.[18]

The first two models account for 85% to 90% of the cases reported in the Mintzberg and Nutt studies cited earlier. For the remaining cases, managers used the Creative Model. In this model the manager takes a fresh look at the problem. He or she is a divergent thinker, and new ideas are sought without regard to what others are doing. Typically, theorists have recommended generating and detailing multiple options. In practice, however, this does not happen. Generally, due to time constraints and high development costs, only one custom-made solution is fully designed. Perhaps it is impractical to develop more than one or two creative solutions. However, you can generate a very large number of skeletal ideas using creative techniques. You can later screen these and then detail the one or two most promising ones.

In summary, managers or teams:
- Often ignore diagnosis completely.
- Often jump to conclusions about causes.
- Formulate and evaluate diagnoses on political or social factors.
- Generate, screen, and flesh out ideas simultaneously.
- Generate few alternatives that are clones of one another and of present practice.
- Promote pet solutions by finding "problems."

Now we know what not to do. Next, we will turn to improving diagnosis, perhaps the most critical of the problem-solving activities.

DIAGNOSIS AS CAUSE ANALYSIS

KEPNER AND TREGOE METHOD	CRITICAL/CONVERGENT
ALTERNATIVE WORLDVIEW METHOD	CREATIVE/DIVERGENT

The Case of the Blackened Filament. These events took place in a large, well-managed plant making plastic filament for textiles.[19] The plant had six banks of machines that produced plastic filaments from viscose raw material. A single bank consisted of a forming machine, an acid bath, 480 lead channels, and 480 revolving buckets. Each forming machine produced 480 gossamer strands of viscose. The strands were drawn along 480 lead channels into an acid bath where they were hardened into plastic filament. The plastic strands were then drawn along additional lead channels and pulleys to 480 individually motorized, revolving buckets. A hood over each acid bath vented the acid fumes to the outside. There was one operator for each machine bank (see Exhibit 5-2).

EXHIBIT 5-2
Diagram of the Filament-making Process—Machine Bank #1

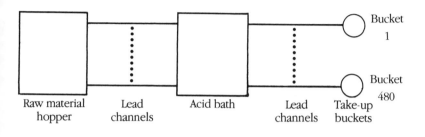

Raw material hopper   Lead channels   Acid bath   Lead channels   Take-up buckets   Bucket 1   Bucket 480

Much like the mud pies we made as youngsters, a filament cake formed in each of the 480 buckets. Due to centrifugal force, the cake grew from the outside wall toward the center of the bucket. When a bucket was full, the operator "doffed it": shut off the motor for bucket #1, cut the filament strand, removed the bucket lid, emptied the bucket filled with plastic filament, replaced the bucket on the motor, reattached the cut filament strand to the bucket, replaced the bucket lid, and restarted the motor. This took exactly one minute. The operator then repeated this procedure as he emptied all 480 buckets during his shift. Hardly job enrichment! Since it took eight hours to form a filament cake, bucket #1 was ready for doffing at the beginning of each shift—and the entire process was then repeated.

Early one morning, trouble came. On the midnight shift, the operator on machine #1 emptied bucket #232 and noticed something strange. There was black filament instead of translucent filament at the center of the filament cake. He did not stop to wonder about it, however, and went on to empty the next bucket a minute later. Again he saw that there was even more blackened plastic at the center of the filament cake. When the operator emptied bucket #242 he noticed that although there was a ring of black filament in the cake, the filament at the center of the cake was again translucent (Exhibit 5-3).

The filament was supposed to be totally translucent; it was partially black. Since the center of the filament was translucent in bucket #242, it appeared that the problem had stopped temporarily. However, since the operator had taken no corrective action, it could reoccur at any time. What had happened? How would you proceed? What questions would you ask? Take a few minutes and develop a list before reading on.

EXHIBIT 5-3
Top-down View of Several Filament Cakes in the Buckets

Translucent
filament
cake

Bucket #232

Filament
cake is
black at
center

Bucket #240

Black
ring but
translucent
at center

Bucket #242

Managers in my problem-solving workshops usually ask the following questions:

1. *Question:* Can we check the acid bath? Is the pH and temperature within acceptable limits?

   Response: Both pH and temperature are within normal limits.

2. *Question:* Has the firm changed its suppliers of raw material lately?

   Response: No.

3. *Question:* Has there been a power outage?

   Response: No.

4. *Question:* Is the operator on machine #1 disgruntled or inept?

   Response: No, he is quite "gruntled" and "ept."

5. *Question:* Let's check the lids of the rubber buckets from #232 to #241. Perhaps the black rubber is flaking off onto the filaments.

   Response: There is no deterioration of the lids.

While my seminar participants ask many questions, most are *implied* solutions. They are jumping to a variety of conclusions. Some think the worker is the cause (question 4); some think that changes in the environment caused the problem (questions 1, 3, and 5); a third group thinks that external factors caused the problem (question 2). All are jumping to conclusions.

Aren't their questions still useful because they are ruling out possible causes? If there were only a few possible causes, this strategy would work. However, when there are a million-and-one possible causes, you must clearly define the problem first. Otherwise, implied solutions only reduce the number of possible causes to a million. That is still too big a search area.

An alternative to the implied solution question is the *diagnostic question.* Your goal is to obtain more information about the deviation between what is and what was. Then you will be in a position to diagnose the causes.

The Kepner and Tregoe Method

The Kepner and Tregoe Method (K-T) transforms an ambiguous mess of symptoms, facts, and assumptions into a clear statement of the causes of a disturbance problem. The K-T Method begins with a blank page. You make no assumptions about the causes; you let the data speak for itself. You develop a diagnosis by answering the following questions:

- *What* is the deviation (versus what it is not)?
- *When* did the deviation occur (versus when it did not occur)?
- *Where* did the deviation occur (versus where it did not occur)?
- *How much, how many, to what extent* did the deviation occur (versus to what extent it did not occur)?
- *Who* is associated with the deviation (versus who is not associated with the deviation)?

The key words are *who, what, where, when,* and *how much.* A reporter would use these words in covering a story. His job is to get the facts. In diagnosing a problem, you must be the honest reporter. What word is missing from our key words?— *Why.* And why is "why" missing? Because, before you have investigated the problem, it does not make sense to ask "why"— you simply do not have enough information to make an intelligent guess. In asking why, we are no longer reporting, we are editorializing. Avoid this in defining the problem.

As you obtain answers to the diagnostic questions, you fill in the worksheet shown in Exhibit 5-4. First let's focus on the first two columns. Here we analyze the problem and seek to understand it better. The first question (*What is* and *What is not*) helps us to distinguish exactly what the problem is. In the blackened filament case, all we now know is that we are getting some black filaments on buckets #232 to #242. But exactly what is the black substance? Is it lead, rubber, grease, and so forth? We do not yet know. *Where* in the production process was the black filament first noticed? Have machines #2 to #6 reported any problems? Where also means the location on the object that has experienced the problem. That is, exactly where on the filament is the blackening? Is it in the interior of a filament, around the entire perimeter, or around only a portion of the perimeter? Clearly location makes a difference as we seek to determine the problem's causes. We also need to know exactly *when* the problem started and stopped? Next we need to know the *extent* of the problem. How many buckets have black filaments? When we emptied bucket #1 some 242 minutes ago it contained only translucent filament. Has any black filament entered bucket #1 in the past four hours? What about buckets #100 or #480? How heavy a layer is the blackening agent? Is the blackening problem increasing, decreasing, or staying the same? Is there a pattern? Has the problem ever happened before? If so, has it happened only on one shift or in one machine bank? And finally, *who* is associated with the problem? Which individual(s) or group(s) is involved with the problem? We are not asking who or what caused the problem, for we are not ready for that yet. In obtaining information to complete the first two columns, please use the following hints:

1. Avoid the use of adjectives in developing entries for the worksheet. If you cannot avoid an adjective, do more detective work and then replace it with a noun.

2. Use wording that avoids double meaning. For example, avoid "not working right" as an entry, since this phrase can take on many meanings.

3. Put as much emphasis in developing entries for the *Is not* column as for the *Is* column.

4. Avoid working on columns 3 and 4 before completing the first two columns.

Adjectives are vague and fuzzy. A diagnosis requires clarity and specificity. Avoid placing adjectives in the completed worksheet. In the Blackened Filament Case we initially defined the problem as blackened filament. You must now conduct tests to determine exactly what the blackening agent is. Until you do this, you have violated rule 1. If avoiding adjectives is critical, then describing a problem as "it is not working the way it is supposed to be" must also be avoided. With that definition you have just scaled Mt. Confusion. The logic behind the last two rules will become clear when we discuss columns 3 and 4 of the worksheet.

Let's return to the Blackened Filament Case. The first two columns of the completed worksheet are shown in Exhibit 5-5.

Our initial worksheet might have included the term *black filament* for the what is entry. However, this violates the first rule. Thus

EXHIBIT 5-4
Kepner and Tregoe Worksheet

	Is	Is not	Any changes that explain entries in first two columns	What is distinctive about entries
What				
Where On object? In space?				
When				
Extent How much? How many? Trend? Pattern?				
Who				

EXHIBIT 5-5
**The Case of the Blackened Filament:
First Two Columns of the Kepner and Tregoe Worksheet**

	Is	*Is not*
What	Carbon	Other blackening agents such as lead, rubber, or grease
Where	On machine #1 Spotted after the acid bath Around one-third of perimeter of the filament	Machines #2–#6 Not spotted before the acid bath In the interior of the filament or around the entire perimeter of the filament
When	Started at minute 232 and ended at minute 241	Before minute 232 or after minute 241
Extent	All 480 buckets of machine #1	Only buckets #232–#241
Who	Machine #1 operator	Operators on other machines

we conducted a lab test. The blackening agent is carbon, not lead or rubber. Then we asked the operator on machine #1 where he first noticed the black filament in the production process. He told us when he emptied bucket #232. On cross examination he told us that as he emptied subsequent buckets he did see black filament *before it entered the buckets.* That is, he remembered seeing black filament in the lead channels between the acid bath and the take-up buckets. He did not notice black filament before the acid bath. Furthermore, no other operators reported any black filament on their machines. To determine the "on the object" entry, we physically examined a filament strand. The carbon was not in the interior of the strand. Rather, it was deposited on about one-third of the filament's perimeter as shown here in a cross-section diagram of a filament in a lead channel:

The problem occurred over a ten-minute period between 3:52 A.M. and 4:01 A.M. (which corresponds to minutes 232 to 241 of the midnight shift). To determine the extent of entry, we checked the other buckets on machine #1. When we emptied bucket #231, there was no black filament. One minute later, there was black filament in bucket #232. However, did black filament enter any of the other buckets from 3:52 A.M. to 4:01 A.M.? Yes. Every bucket on machine #1 had black filament in it during the ten-minute period.

Our analysis has yielded the following problem statement:

> What factor or factors could cause carbon on all 480 filament cakes on only machine #1? The carbon problem occurred between 3:52 A.M. and 4:01 A.M. The carbon was first noticed between the acid bath and the take-up buckets. The carbon did not penetrate the interior of the filament but was deposited on one-third of the filament's perimeter. Only the operator on machine #1 is involved.

This definition is clearly better than "we have some black filament on some of the buckets of machine #1." A precise problem definition helps to narrow the search for causes. The problem statement suggests that carbon floated down and deposited itself on all the filaments of machine #1. You may find that your eyes are drawn to the ceiling area over the acid bath, lead channels, and take-up buckets. Now you are ready for cause analysis.

The problem statement also destroys the causes offered earlier. The acid bath cannot be at fault since the acid would disintegrate carbon. But carbon is on the filament. Thus, the problem must have happened after the acid bath. We do not have a raw material problem, because in that case the carbon would most likely be in the interior of the filament. We can reject a power outage since that could not produce carbon. The operator cannot be the cause. How could he place carbon in all 480 buckets while the machine was in operation? And, finally, the cause cannot be the rubber buckets—the blackening agent is carbon, not rubber.

All these implied solutions were wrong. The major problem was that our managers were "solution-minded." They wanted to solve the problem before they knew what it was. Well, now we know. Now we are ready to determine the causes. Here we use columns 3 and 4 of the worksheet. Restating rule 4: *Hold off on assessing causes until you understand the problem.*

We ask ourselves two questions. What planned or unplanned changes in personnel, task, or the environment have happened recently that might explain an *Is* and a corresponding *Is not* entry? What changes could explain the presence of carbon, the particular ten-minute segment, or that the problem happened only on machine #1? You should also ask, what is unique about an *Is* versus an *Is not* entry? What is distinctive about machine #1, carbon in contrast to lead or rubber, or that all 480 buckets on machine #1 had black filament? Write down all the changes and distinctions you can generate. Do not try to prove a pet solution. Let the data speak for itself. Your chances of completing the last two columns increase if you have completed the first two columns. If you ignore the *Is not* entries, you make potential cause assessment more difficult.

Exhibit 5-6 contains columns 3 and 4 for the Case of the Blackened Filament.

EXHIBIT 5-6
The Case of the Blackened Filament:
Last Two Columns of the Kepner and Tregoe Worksheet

Columns 1–2	Changes	Unique
Carbon	??	No source of carbon in the plant.
Machine #1	None made	Unique operator, physical location within the plant, hood over acid bath.
After acid bath	??	Rules out raw material or source of problem before acid bath.
On exposed perimeter	??	Carbon falling like snowflakes from above.
3:52 A.M.–4:01 A.M.	??	
All 480 buckets	??	There is a common cause.

The manager could not think of changes that could explain the *Is/Is not* entries. However, the unique column suggested looking outside the plant for the carbon source. There were plenty of carbon sources outside the plant—smokestacks and coal-burning train engines. But how had the carbon entered the plant and "snowed" only on machine #1? The carbon source could not be the ceiling. Lead-based paints were used for the ceilings. The hood above the acid bath was the only other possible source of entry. Each machine had its own vent to draw acid fumes to the outside. That might explain why the carbon did not affect the other five machines. Plant personnel checked machine #1's vent and found traces of carbon in the ductwork. Moreover, the vent fan was not working. Now they knew how the carbon had entered the plant; they still did not know its source. First they thought of the smokestacks. Each day at noon, the stacks were cleared, and a large cloud of carbon was emitted into the air. However, that had happened some 15 hours earlier. The timing was not right. But they noticed that there was a railroad siding below the point where machine #1 was vented to the outside. They checked with the rail yard dispatcher and discovered that a train had been parked at the siding at about 4:00 A.M. They also discovered that the engineer had cleared the train's smokestacks during the ten-minute period. Apparently a cloud of carbon entered the hood's ductwork because the fan was not working. Most of the carbon fell harmlessly into the acid bath. Some, however, fell onto the filaments between the acid bath and the take-up buckets.

Use columns 3 and 4 to help you seek and evaluate possible causes. If a team member offers a possible solution, you can quickly evaluate it. The greater the number of column 1 and 2 entries that a potential cause explains, the greater the likelihood that it is the correct cause. Forget those causes that agree with only a few entries. Investigate the others.

The moral of the story: do not jump to conclusions. Diagnose the problem, develop a problem statement, and then generate, investigate, and evaluate possible causes.

The Case of the Burred Panels. A plant makes two types of hood panels for cars.[20] Metal sheets are first cut into identical-size blanks and are stacked 40 to a pallet. The pallets are then delivered to a stamping operation. Here stamping presses shape the blanks into hood panels. There is always a supply of blanks for the operators of the four stamping presses at 8 A.M., the beginning of the day shift. The stamping operators use the starter supply while they wait for the morning shift to produce more blanks. The Panther and Cheetah panels differ in only one respect—the depth of draw, or curvature, of the panels after the stamping operation.

Lines 1 and 2 stamp 80 Panther panels (deep draw) per hour. Line 4 stamps 50 Panther panels per hour, and line 3 stamps 80 Cheetah (shallow draw) panels per hour. All except line 2 have four pallets of blanks at the beginning of the morning shift. Line 2 workers have complained that, with only two stacks, they sometimes have to stop and wait for the morning shift to produce more blanks for stamping. They have demanded equal treatment with the other lines.

On Wednesday at 11:00 A.M., the plant manager calls an emergency meeting. This morning at about 9:30 A.M. the stamping press on line 2 started producing nearly 12% rejects. After the morning break at 10 A.M., the stamping press on line 1 also started producing about 12% rejects; the normal rate is under 2%. The problem is excessive burrs and other rough spots. The manager reports that the engineering department has not found anything wrong with the four presses.

Several supervisors argue that sabotage may be the problem. Everyone agrees that the workers could cause excessive burrs by mispositioning a blank in the press. Moreover, the day before, the supervisor on line 2 had dismissed a worker for allegedly drinking on the job. When the worker returned this morning, the supervisor again confronted him and demanded an apology. For 30 minutes they argued while the workers on line 2 watched from the sidelines. Finally, the supervisor fired the worker. The union has threatened to file a grievance. Another supervisor wonders if an injury to a dock worker on the previous midnight shift is related to the problem. His forklift tipped over trying to move a raw material shipment to the blanking operation. The firm had recently switched to Zenith Metals Company as their raw materials supplier. Zenith's method of shipping raw material differed from that of the previous supplier. Being unaware of this, the dock worker had suffered a slight injury. No one else feels that the two incidents are related. During the meeting the group learns that at 11:20 A.M. the stamping press on line 4 also started producing about 12% rejects. Only line 3, which is run by the most respected supervisor, is not experiencing any excessive rejects yet.

At the end of the meeting, the plant manager believes he has only two options: (1) to back up his supervisor and not reinstate the dismissed worker, or (2) to reinstate the dismissed worker. With the former option, he runs the risk of a wildcat strike and, perhaps, continued excessive burrs. With the latter option, he runs the risk of demoralizing his supervisory staff. He has assumed that the dismissed worker and the burred panels are related. Are they? Before reading on, please develop the first two columns of the Kepner and Tregoe worksheet (Exhibit 5-7).

EXHIBIT 5-7
The Case of the Burred Panels:
First Two Columns of the Kepner and Tregoe Worksheet

	Is	*Is not*
What	Burrs and nicks on quarter panels	Other finishing or materials problems, such as ripples or soft spots
Where	On lines 1, 2, and 4 On object: ???	Line 3 At blanking operation
When	Line 1: at 10:15 A.M. Line 2: at 9:30 A.M. Line 4: at 11:20 A.M.	Never before
Extent	Line 1, 2, and 4 producing about 12% rejects Reject rate constant for past several hours	Line 3 producing 2% rejects
Who	Operators on lines 1, 2, and 4	Operators on line 3

We almost have sufficient data for a complete problem statement. However, we do not know the exact location of the nicks and burrs. Are they randomly distributed over an entire panel? Or are they all located in one area on each panel? An investigation will reveal that all burrs and nicks are at the center of each panel. We can now develop a formal problem definition:

> What factor or factors caused burrs on about 12% of the panels on lines 1, 2, and 4? There are no problems at the blanking operation or the line 3 stamping presses. Line 2 started producing 12% rejects at 9:30 A.M.; line 1 started producing 12% rejects at 10:15 A.M.; and line 4 started producing 12% rejects at 11:20 A.M. All burrs are at the center of the panels.

Perhaps the most obvious cause is the dismissed worker. But let's not jump to conclusions. Rather, we should begin by seeking distinctions and looking for other changes. What is distinctive about lines 1, 2, and 4? In comparison to line 3, the workers have less respect for their supervisors. Also, these three lines produce the Panther, or deep draw, panel. Have there been any other changes recently that might explain the problem? Yes, today the firm started using Zenith Metals. Thus there are two plausible explanations: a sabotage, or a raw material problem.

We use the other K-T entries to help us determine the likelihood of each cause. Which cause better explains why line 2, then line 1, and then line 4 started producing 12% rejects? What might explain the exact times? Also, which potential cause better explains why the nicks are all at the center of the panels?

If the sabotage hypothesis is true, the workers on line 2 must have told the others of the dismissal during the break. This might explain why lines 1 and 4 started producing rejects after the morning break. However, sabotage is unlikely to have caused all the nicks at the center of each panel. We would expect the location of the burrs to vary from panel to panel.

Is the Zenith hypothesis more plausible? The blanks on the morning pallets were from the old supplier. Line 2 produces 80 units per hour. They had two stacks of 40 blanks. Given the half-hour fracas as the beginning of the shift, they would have run out of old material at 9:30 A.M. The increased reject rate coincides with the use of Zenith blanks. The Zenith hypothesis also explains the timing of line 1 and 4. But why were there no problems on the Cheetah line? In producing a deep draw, the metal cracked at the point of greatest depth—the center of the panel. There were no excessive burrs on the Cheetah panels because less pressure was needed to form those panels. Thus the Zenith metal did not crack.

The dismissed worker and the burred panels are not related. The cause is the Zenith metals. The plant manager must still decide what to do about the dismissed worker. However, he now knows that whatever he does will not affect the burred panels problem.

ALTERNATIVE WORLDVIEW METHOD

In the Kepner and Tregoe (K-T) Method we make no assumptions about causality. Beginning with a blank page, we seek data to define the problem. Only then do we begin to search for causes. This is a powerful diagnostic technique, but it is not suitable for everyone. We may find it difficult to restrain our natural tendency to seek causes.

Selective perception influences cause assessment. Marketing managers view problems as marketing problems. Operations managers view the same problems as production problems. That is not all. Often managers attribute causes to others or to factors beyond their control. Workers attribute problems to changes in management practice, to the job, or to the external environment. Managers attribute the same problems to the workers, or to uncontrollable changes in the job or the external environment. This tendency to immediately look for causes is counterproductive. But that is the way we are. The Alternative Worldview Method recognizes this and improves our natural tendencies.

The Alternative Worldview Method helps those who cannot cope with the blank-page concept. You form subgroups and ask each group to examine different possible causes. The subgroups should seek supporting data for their views. Then, in a structured debate, each subgroup presents its evidence and discusses the merits of each view. Now the team as a whole selects one view, develops a synthesis view, or generates a new view of the cause(s).

The Alternative Worldview Method is successful because it helps us do what we naturally do best—seek causes. However, it structures the process to minimize the negative consequences of jumping to conclusions or selective perception. The Alternative Worldview Method accepts us for what we are and makes incremental changes in how we diagnose problems. The K-T Method helps us to act more normatively by requiring revolutionary changes in practice.

The following diagram captures the major philosophical difference in how each method searches for causes:

Kepner and Tregoe   Alternative Worldview

The K-T Method is a convergent process. You start with a blank page, and as you answer the diagnostic questions, you reduce the search area for possible causes. After completing the worksheet for the burred-panels case, we had narrowed the problem down to two possible causes. The Alternative Worldview Method causes you to diverge *initially*. You analyze several plausible causes, and then through analysis and comparison you converge to the true causes(s).

One final difference is the intended audience. The K-T Method is an individual problem-solving tool, while the Alternative Worldview Method is a group problem-solving tool. Teams can, however, use the K-T Method in conjunction with the Nominal Group Technique. Ask each team member to generate an initial worksheet. Each member then presents a worksheet and a brief defense of the entries. No discussion is permitted during the round-robin. Afterward, team members reconcile any differences there may be. While groups can use the K-T Method, they are essential for the Alternative Worldview Method. You must form subgroups, have each analyze different problem causes, and then reach a consensus.

The dialectic process underlies the Alternative Worldview Method. Dialectic logicians propose that for any position or thesis there is an alternative, incompatible position, or antithesis. Unfortunately, the nature of the antithesis is not always clear:

> Now in Kant's "Transcendal Dialectic," the antithesis was found in a straightforward logical manner. If the thesis is, "The world had a beginning in time," the antithesis is "The world had no beginning in time." . . . In Hegel, on the other hand, the antithesis is not the contradictor of the thesis, but rather its deadliest enemy. . . . The deadliest enemy concept is found most clearly in politics. The deadliest enemy of democracy is not non-democracy but a very explicit and detailed political design call the Communist Party.[21]

Hegel's perspective is more relevant for problem diagnosis. What is the deadliest enemy of the position that workers are the cause of a problem? Rather than say that it is not the workers, we need to be very explicit. The enemy might be changes in the task or the organization's structure. It might be factors outside of the firm. It might be changes in management practice.

The Alternative Worldview Method uses four generic causes:

• *Internal Cause*—Causes of the problem lie with actions (or lack of actions) taken within the department, organization, or industry. We view the causes as errors of omission or commission that happened "inside." The problem's causes are due to *controllable* factors.

• *External Cause*—Causes of the problem lie with the inability to deal with factors over which we have little or no control. We view the causes as errors of omission or commission that happened "outside." The problem's causes are due to *uncontrollable* factors.

• *Human Causes*—Causes of a problem evolve from individuals who either took no action or the wrong action. Included are failures to communicate, motivate, lead, or envision. The problem's causes are interpersonal or managerial.

• *Technological Causes*—Causes of the problem lie with the failure of systems, processes, structures, or procedures. No systems (structures) or improper systems are in place. The problem's causes are *structural*.

As leader, you subdivide your team into two or more subgroups. You either assign a subgroup to a generic cause or have them select one of the causes. It is not necessary to assign subgroups to all four causes. But the team must consider at least two different worldviews (Human versus Technological, or Internal versus External).

Consider how the Alternative Worldview Method might address the following problem: Recently, job-related accidents have increased significantly, and the workers are threatening a job action. Four subgroups independently analyze the problem along one of the four generic causes. Each searches for hard data to support its position. The *internal* cause subgroup proposes that management has not installed the proper safety equipment on the machines. The *external* cause subgroup proposes that the national union is asking the local body to report every accident as a bargaining chip in the upcoming negotiations. The *human* cause subgroup proposes that workers are unwilling to learn how to operate the new equipment; they are resisting change. The *technological* cause subgroup proposes that the increased accidents are due to the new production equipment—the vendor or company did not offer sufficient training to the operators, or the industrial engineering group failed to conduct extensive pilot studies before installing the equipment.

Now the entire team can meet in a plenary session. The four views are compared and evaluated, and in a structured debate, the team determines the cause(s).

Perhaps the following anecdote will further clarify the generic cause definitions.

The Case of the Missing Information. This story takes place in a marketing department of a large industrial organization. Many of the marketing managers complained that they did not have the necessary information to make effective decisions in introducing new products. They had never complained before. Sensing that the company had an important problem, the CEO contacted the information systems group. Information systems, of course, chose to define the causes as *technological.* The group proposed three alternative computerized systems. Each was very expensive and required extensive user training.

Although the CEO had some misgivings, he implemented one of the recommended systems. The marketing managers showed little enthusiasm for the system during its six-month installation. However, the CEO hoped that once the system was in place it would be used.

This did not happen. One year later, few managers were using the computer system. Less than 50% had even attended the training sessions. Moreover, the system had no impact on the marketing managers' decision making. And they still complained that they needed more information.

Perhaps the problem was not technological. The CEO had not considered that he was facing a *human* problem. He asked a psychologist who worked for corporate planning to interview the marketing managers. The psychologist concluded that the problem was not a lack of information; rather, managers were apprehensive about making risky decisions involving huge sums of money. Over the past several years the cost of introducing a new product had skyrocketed. The marketing managers realized that any mistake would be costly to them and to the firm. Viewing it as a human problem, the psychologist offered two solutions: (1) modify the reward system to emphasize long-term performance or (2) require groups of managers rather than just a single product manager to sign off on product introduction decisions.

The CEO tried the "share the risk" approach. The results were astonishing. Marketing managers became more enthusiastic and sought creative ways to promote their products. The lack of information complaint never surfaced again.

The moral of the story: *Solve the right problem.* Developing and evaluating alternative causes is the key to a divergent diagnostic strategy. Remember, almost any solution to the right problem beats the best solution to the wrong problem. A correct diagnosis is essential.

Before applying the Alternative Worldview Method to another case, here are some guidelines:

• Your cause should guide your investigation. Seek data that are consistent with your cause.

• Do not prematurely commit to your cause. Do not become emotionally attached to your position. Remember, the goal is to create and resolve doubt as to the true cause. Truly suspend judgment until you have completed the structured debate. If you cannot tolerate doubt, do not use the Alternative Worldview Method.

• Do not ignore negative evidence. It is more impressive than affirmative evidence. During the structured debate, drop an unsupported cause.

A. H. Robins and the Robaxyn Dilemma. Recently A. H. Robins, a pharmaceutical firm, has been in the news. They produced and distributed the Dalkon Shield and are facing one of the largest class action suits ever filed. While the courts have not ruled on the case, the firm has sought Chapter 11 protection against bankruptcy. Robins, however, has encountered other crises.

In 1958 a chemist at Robins synthesized a petroleum-based chemical called methocarbomal, a muscle relaxant. As Robins made only finished pharmaceuticals at that time, contracts for making the raw methocarbomal were given to several chemical companies. The muscle relaxant, which sold in pill form under the name Robaxyn, was a big success.

In 1967 Robins believed that it was buying enough methocarbomal to consider making the chemical itself. This was especially attractive because the company also purchased large volumes of glyceryl guaiacolate (GG) for its cough medicine products. As methocarbomal was a derivative of GG, manufacturing the two chemicals seemed desirable.

Robins temporarily shelved their plans when the Food and Drug Administration's Drug Efficacy Study in 1970 gave methocarbomal a "questionable" rating. In 1974 the FDA removed this rating.

Meanwhile the 1973 oil embargo made it difficult for Robins to get methocarbomal and GG. Furthermore, the price of methocarbomal shot up by more than 40% in 1974. Thus, Robins again considered producing methocarbomal. The company also considered two other options: to acquire an existing production plant, or to use prudent hedging operations that would allow them to buy supplies when prices were low.

After much study, Robins decided to build its own plant. Then, at the last minute, the company was offered an opportunity to enter into a joint venture with a German pharmaceutical firm to produce methocarbomal. Robins chose this option because it reduced the company's capital spending outlays and seemed to provide a reasonable solution.[22]

What exactly was Robins's problem? Clearly one problem was how to react to the methocarbomal and GG shortages they now faced. But there may have been others. It appears that the Robins management had not diagnosed the *complete* problem. Rather, they generated alternative options to the most obvious problem. Therefore, while the methocarbomal shortage problem was critical, it may have masked a more insidious problem.

Two groups of managers recently analyzed this problem using the Alternative Worldview Method. The external perspective subgroup highlighted the following data in their cause analysis:

• Robins was at the mercy of multiple suppliers of methocarbomal and GG.

• Because of the 1973 oil embargo, methocarbomal and GG were either not available or only available at very high costs.

• The economy was suffering from stagflation.

• The FDA took four years to rule on the questionable rating.

The external subgroup concluded that the causes were due to factors beyond Robins's control. What Robins must do is to make the best of a bad situation. Their goal should be to stabilize their supply of raw material and protect themselves from escalating costs. Robins's management team *implicitly* arrived at the same conclusion.

The internal subgroup highlighted the following data in their analysis:

• Robins's management was unsure of what type of firm it wanted to be: a vertically integrated firm or a finished pharmaceutical house.

• Senior management's decision-making processes were slow and reactive. Management took no decisive action between 1967 and 1970.

• The firm appeared to have no effective long-range planning process in place to monitor political events (the FDA ruling) or any contingency plans either.

The team concluded that the causes were due to failures in long-range planning and indecisive decision making. Robins's management must assume some responsibility for the situation.

Each subgroup now presented its evidence in a structured debate using the Nominal Group Technique. Both subgroups quickly agreed that the major cause was Robins's indecisiveness and reactive decision-making processes. However, they agreed that the oil embargo was directly responsible for the company's higher costs and unreliable supply problems. The team proposed a short-term and a long-term solution. In the short run, Robins must consider alternative ways to ensure a steady supply of methocarbomal. The team suggested obtaining long-term contracts for petroleum with domestic or non-OPEC suppliers. Longer term, Robins must establish an effective long-range planning group.

It might have been difficult for Robins's own management to conclude that they were part of the problem. Yet, if we start with the premise that internal factors can cause a problem, and we make a strong case, then perhaps we can overcome the tendency to blame others. To paraphrase Shakespeare, when looking for causes, don't look to the stars. Often the fault lies within ourselves.

Which method—K-T or Alternative Worldview—should you use? As both are effective, the choice boils down to your personal preferences—convergent or divergent; which technique has worked for you in the past; the scope of problem; or whether you are working alone or with a team.

DIAGNOSIS AS PROBLEM OR GOAL REFORMULATION

PROBLEM BOUNDARY EXPANSION	CREATIVE/DIVERGENT
5Ws METHOD	CREATIVE/DIVERGENT

The K-T and Alternative Worldview methods are useful when seeking causes. For a disturbance problem, knowing the cause is often equivalent to solving the problem. If the fan in the textile plant is not working, replace it. Other times, there are multiple ways to proceed. Should our goal be to replace Zenith Metals, change the manufacturing process to accommodate Zenith Metals, or use multiple raw material suppliers? Your ultimate alternatives depend on which goal you select.

Goal reformulation is hardly a new concept. After the Revolutionary War, the 13 states nearly fell apart under the Articles of Confederation. These granted ultimate power to the states and made it difficult to forge a nation. The nation's debts multiplied and anarchy reigned. In Massachusetts, Captain Daniel Shay led an armed rebellion. General Washington called a meeting at Annapolis, but several states were too skeptical to even send delegates. The meeting dragged on with few results. Then Alexander Hamilton restructured the goal. Rather than attempt to salvage the Articles of Confederation, he proposed building a new governmental structure. His goal restructuring led to the adoption of our present Constitution in 1787.

It is all in how you define the problem. For most entrepreneurial problems there is not a single "correct" definition. While some definitions are broader in scope, others are very narrow. Each provides a different view of the problem. In the Japanese play *Rashamon*, each character recalls an encounter with bandits along the roadside. All see the same encounter quite differently. None are right and all are right. Similarly, there is no one best problem statement. All provide different goals which, in turn, help you generate different solutions.

While useful for disturbance problems, restructuring is essential in diagnosing entrepreneurial problems. To restructure, you can either change your point of view or change your goals or objectives.[23] Changing your viewpoint means asking, "how do others see the problem?" You have already learned a strategy to do this. Include multiple stakeholders on your team. Each brings a different perspective, and ensures that your team will consider alternative goals. Remember the MARTA Committee of 50!

Problem Boundary Expansion

Problem Boundary Expansion produces different goals. In turn, these goals help you generate radically different solutions. We begin with an initial goal statement that includes an action verb, an object phrase, and an optional qualifying phrase.[24]

In 1787, the delegates at the Annapolis meeting might have formulated the original problem as:

To improve (action verb)	*the Articles of Confederation* (object phrase)	*within three months* (qualifying phrase)

Begin with the initial formulation and use the following *transition phrases* to develop a second formulation.

START: I want (Goal Formulation #1)

TRANSITION PHRASES:
                    in order
                    in such a way as

Now you have Goal Formulation #2. Again use the transition phrase to develop a third formulation.

I want (Goal Formulation #2)
                    in order
                    in such a way as

Now you have Goal Formulation #3, and so forth.

You continue to reformulate the problem using the transition phrases. After several iterations, you review the alternative goals and decide which one or ones to pursue.

Let's return to the Annapolis meeting. The delegates are frustrated with their lack of progress. Hamilton proposes using the Problem Boundary Expansion Method. He begins with the original purpose of the meeting.

We want	[to improve the Articles of Confederation within three months]
in order	[to preserve the Union]
We want	[to preserve the Union]
in such a way as	[to maintain individual rights while developing a national unity]
We want	[to maintain individual rights . . .]
in order	[to promote the welfare of all]

Now the delegates have four different goals. Improving the Articles of Confederation is different from maintaining individual rights while developing a national unity. Each suggests somewhat different solutions. And that is the purpose of goal redefinition. Remember, the best solution to the wrong problem will not work.

The Parking Space Assignment Case. You have recently been appointed manager of a new division that will be housed in a building presently under construction. Your team of five department heads has been selected, and they are working with you in selecting their own staffs, purchasing office equipment, and generally anticipating the problems that are likely to arise when you move into the new building four months from now.

Yesterday you received from the architect a final set of plans for the building. For the first time, you examined the available parking facilities. There is a large lot across the street intended for clerical and blue-collar personnel and for lower-level managers. In addition, there are ten spaces immediately adjacent to the building intended for visitors and reserved parking. Company policy requires a minimum of six spaces for visitor parking. This leaves only four spaces to allocate among you and your five managers. There is no room to increase the size of this parking lot.

Up to now, your senior management team has worked very well together;

they have felt part of a close-knit team. To be sure, there are salary and seniority differences among your staff. However, each has recently been promoted into his or her new job and expects reserved parking privileges as a consequence of their new status. From past experience you know that people feel strongly about things that reflect their status within the company. You are reluctant to do anything that will jeopardize the special team relationship that has developed. Nevertheless, you must allocate four reserved parking spaces among yourself and your five managers.[25]

Let's begin with the most obvious definition:

I want   [to assign six managers to four available parking spaces].

Before continuing, try reformulating the above goal set using Problem Boundary Expansion. Managers at a recent workshop generated the following alternative goals:

- To maintain the esprit de corps of the management team.
- To award for best performance, seniority, etc.
- To improve the morale of the entire work force.
- To minimize status differences.
- To have all team members enthusiastically endorse the assignment.

Each goal suggests alternative solutions that might have been overlooked by the initial problem statement. With Problem Boundary Expansion you can clearly see the tight connection between goals and solutions. They are different sides of the same coin.

The 5Ws Method

Developed by Arthur VanGundy, the 5Ws Method is a comprehensive redefinitional method.[26] Here you apply probing questions to the initial goal. You ask who, what, where, when, and why questions. Team members should ask as many different questions as they can for each of the Ws. The more questions they ask, the more information they generate for alternative goals. To maximize new information, members should underline and focus on key words in the initial definition. Let's apply the 5Ws Method to the following scenario.

The Sick Leave Problem. The management of a firm determines that, based on industry data, their workers are abusing the sick leave privilege.

Management's goal is to reduce sick leave usage to the industry average. Their initial goal is: How can we *motivate workers* to use less *sick leave*?

Key words have been italicized. Now the management team used these words to frame the following probing questions:

Question	Answer
Who are the workers?	They are blue-collar workers. They work in unpleasant environments.
Who needs to be motivated?	Workers who use sick leave and are absent a lot.
Who uses sick leave?	Workers who are sick, workers who are bored, or those who have to attend to personal business.
What is motivation?	It is drive, a need to achieve.
Where are workers motivated?	They are motivated at award ceremonies or on the job.
When are workers motivated?	When they peform well, when they are rewarded, or when they feel good about themselves and their work.
When do workers use sick leave?	They use it on Mondays and on Fridays.
Why do workers need to be motivated?	To use less sick leave, to produce more, or to be absent less.
Why do workers use sick leave?	To get well, to complete personal business, or to overcome boredom.

The management team now developed the following alternative goals:

In what ways might working conditions be improved?

In what ways might workers' health be improved?

In what ways might workers be rewarded for working on Mondays and Fridays?

In what ways might workers be paid for being well?

In what ways might workers accomplish personal business without using sick leave?

In what ways might we reduce boredom on the job?

In what ways might we improve workers' self-image?

You get the idea. The information from the probing questions helps to reformulate the goal. Some redefinitions may need further refinement before they can be used to generate solutions. While there is no correct goal, each guides you to different search areas for solutions.

The 5Ws and K-T methods are similar in one respect. With one exception, both ask similar probing questions to generate more information. "Why" is not used in the K-T Method until you have completed the first two columns of the worksheet. In the 5Ws Method we use the answers to redefine the goal. In the K-T Method we use the answers to determine the causes of a problem.

Diagnosis is the most critical phase of problem solving. And we are not especially good at it. However, you must know the causes of a disturbance problem or consider alternative reformulations for disturbance or entrepreneurial problems. Without diagnosis, you will not generate effective solutions. Rotten apples or good ones; the choice is yours.

ALTERNATIVE GENERATION

General Principles

A diagnosed problem is half solved. Now you must generate alternatives, formally evaluate them, and implement your choice. Alternative generation includes designing or seeking skeletal ideas, screening them, and then fleshing out the most promising ones into fully developed solutions.

Before getting to specifics, here are some guiding principles in alternative generation. All attempt to minimize the ineffectual real-world practices discussed earlier:
• Generate six to ten skeletal ideas for discussion.
• In seeking skeletal ideas, see what others—other divisions or competitors—have done in similar situations. If necessary, modify their practices.
• In seeking skeletal ideas, ask vendors, suppliers, or consultants.
• Design at least one skeletal innovative idea. Go beyond the Timid Explorer Model.

- Screen your skeletal ideas.
- Develop at least two detailed solutions for final evaluation.
- When you fail to generate an effective solution, consider rediagnosing the problem or developing or modifying your skeletal ideas.

GENERATING INNOVATIVE SKELETAL IDEAS

NOMINAL GROUP TECHNIQUE	CREATIVE/DIVERGENT
ANALOGY	CREATIVE/DIVERGENT

A skeletal idea is an executive summary or overview that can be written on a single page. It should include a brief description of the idea, its rationale, and very rough estimates of the costs and benefits.

Nominal Group Technique

The Nominal Group Technique is particularly suited to alternative generation. Have each team member silently and independently generate their ideas before the meeting. Then, after the round-robin presentations, ensure that all the ideas are at the same level of detail and specificity. You may also wish to cluster ideas hierarchically and generate several mega-ideas.

During the open discussion period, first seek additional ideas. Look for variations on your original ideas. Try brainstorming. Or take a 30-minute break and again, silently and independently, generate additional ideas. The open discussion may have stimulated members to think along new lines. The silent period helps them to organize and soldify their thoughts into concrete ideas. Your goal is to generate six to ten skeletal ideas.

Use the following principles during the open discussion:
- Critical thinking uber alles.
- Don't proselytize.
- Use a devil's advocate.

- Everyone participates.
- Reality-test ideas.

To further increase your chances of developing different skeletal solutions, your team should include multiple stakeholders, members from different departments, or members with different decision-making styles.

Analogy

If you want more skeletal solutions than the Nominal Group Technique can deliver, consider using the Analogy Method. An analogy is a familiar story with plenty of action. The analogy need not be similar to your problem; the analogy is merely a vehicle that helps to unclog your mind. It helps overcome the mental blocks that keep you from solving the problem. It is a way to generate that all-important moment of insight. It is a way to turn your brain's light bulb on.

Here are four steps for developing skeletal ideas through Analogy:

- Generate an analogy.
- Forget the original problem that is defying solution. Think of ways to solve the problem posed in the analogy. Do not place any constraints on yourself in solving the analogy.
- *Force fit* the analogy solutions. Transfer the analogy solutions to the original problem.
- At *another* meeting, select six to ten solutions for development into one-page executive summaries.

Some of my favorite analogies are: (1) working on a tough crossword puzzle, (2) getting a reluctant cat off of a roof, and (3) getting tickets to an oversold sporting event. Each one of us has experienced these problems. Furthermore, the analogies are action-packed and fun to solve.

Let's apply Analogy to the Parking Space Assignment problem. The goal is: To assign four spaces among six managers.

After a Nominal Group Technique session, a group of eight

managers was given the following analogy to solve: How to get a reluctant cat off a roof in any way they can. Eliminating duplicates, they generated the following list in 15 minutes:

Throw rocks	Tear house down
Shoot the cat	Use a ladder
Starve the cat	Put dog on roof
Throw fishnet on cat	Coax cat with food
Call fire department	Build new building next door
Ignore cat	Spray with water hose
Cut hole in roof	Replace the cat
Scare cat off	Call cat by name
Throw water at cat	Use helicopter
Buzz cat with airplane	Lasso the cat
Call roofers	Bang on ceiling
Set house on fire	Use mouse
Suck up with vacuum	Use catnip
Trampoline and grab cat	Use tranquilizer gun
Set line trap	Swat with long stick
Send up another cat	Give cat and friend a weekend in
Sell building	Las Vegas
Throw small bomb	Throw fire crackers
Pile up dirt to roof	Plant fast-growing tree
Transplant a tree	Dig under house until roof at
Grease the cat	ground level
Grease the roof	Grease the instructor for using this
Wait for tornado	analogy
Bomb the neighborhood	Hire a "hit man or cat"
Call ASCPA (a cat lover)	Give cat lightning rod
Hire cat psychologist	Tempt with caged bird
Play loud music	Tell cat "you can't come down"
Pray	Tell joke, cat listens, and falls off
	the roof

Clearly the group enjoyed themselves. It is also apparent that there were few cat lovers in the group. When the group lost momentum, the instructor suggested they seek variations, reverse their ideas, or combine or modify ideas.

Now the team was ready for the force-fit session. First, the original parking assignment problem statement was restated. The instructor then told them that he would randomly select an analogy solution and that they must, without hesitation, use it to solve the parking space problem. Whatever the analogy solution conjured up in their minds, they must make it work on the parking problem. Idea evaluation was out; this would be done later.

The instructor selected the helicopter solution. Their force fit solutions are shown in Exhibit 5-8. After the session was over, each team member was asked how he or she had made the transfer. Their reasoning is also presented in Exhibit 5-8.

Notice how the same analogy solution generated different ideas. Some members literally transferred the analogy solution to the real problem. Others used the analogy solution as a metaphor, while others found something concrete in the analogy solution to fix on. Irrespective of which method they used, they were able to find a connection.

Remember, one analogy solution generated seven ideas for the Parking Space Assignment problem. Several more analogy solutions were selected for force-fit and the group generated several new ideas. This list differed from the solutions generated by the Nominal Group Technique. And that was the goal—to generate radically different ideas in a short period of time.

EXHIBIT 5-8
**Using an Analogy Solution to Solve
the Parking Space Assignment Problem**

Reasoning process	Solution
Helicopter blades are sharp.	Assign spaces to sharpest workers.
Helicopters create strong winds.	Ask for change in present company policy on need for visitor parking.
Helicopter carries cat off roof.	Build a second level.
Helicopter blades rotate.	Rotate assignment of team members to preferred parking spaces.
Helicopters go straight up.	Have additional parking on roof.
Helicopters need little space to lift off.	Reconfigure lot for compact cars.
Helicopters move fast.	Move the entire management team to a nearby parking lot. Assign preferred spaces within that lot.
Helicopters kick up dust.	Leave latecomers in dust. Assign spots on first-come/first-serve basis.

In another team meeting, the group would have identified the top six to ten contenders.

Your team should be able to generate at least 50 ideas with a good analogy in 15 to 20 minutes. Of course, it depends on the team's makeup (see Chapter 3). Teams with many N-dominant (intuitive) members seem to generate more ideas. N-dominant managers are also able to force-fit the analogy solutions back to the real problem. Teams with extreme S-dominant (sensing) managers may find analogy too far out or just plain silly. Recently, one team of extreme S-dominant managers could not generate more than 20 ideas. And what is worse, they found it difficult to force-fit their ideas. Analogy is not for everyone.

SCREENING SKELETAL IDEAS

NOMINAL GROUP TECHNIQUE	CRITICAL/CONVERGENT
FRANKLIN'S MORAL ALGEBRA	CRITICAL/CONVERGENT

It is impossible to fully develop six to ten alternative solutions. It takes too much time, it costs too much, and it taxes our cognitive abilities. So we must screen our list to identify the two or three best ideas. Make this an explicit activity during your team meeting.

The Nominal Group Technique

Consider using the voting procedure of the Nominal Group Technique. When the group fails to reach a consensus, you ask the members to rank order the skeletal ideas. Of course, the procedure is by silent ballot. In this way you can determine which ideas have the strongest support within the group.

Franklin's Moral Algebra

Over 200 years ago, Benjamin Franklin developed a simple procedure for screening alternatives. Consider the following letter to Joseph Priestly, the discoverer of oxygen. Priestly sought Franklin's advice on a personal matter. Franklin wrote:

In affairs of so much importance to you, wherein you ask my advice, I cannot, for want of sufficient premises, counsel you what to determine; but, if you please, I will tell you how.

When these difficult cases occur, they are difficult, chiefly, because while we have them under consideration, all the reasons pros and cons are not present to the mind at the same time. Hence the various purposes or inclinations that alternatively prevail, and the uncertainty that perplexes us.

To get this over, my way is to divide half of a sheet of paper by a line, into two columns: writing over the one "pro" and over the other "con." Then, during three or four days' consideration, I put down under the different heads, short hints of the different motives that at different times occur to me for or against a measure.

When I have got these together in one view, I endeavor to estimate their respective weights, and where I find two (one on each side) that seem equal, I strike them both out. If I find a reason "pro" equal to some two reasons "con," I strike out the three reasons. If I judge some two reasons "con" equal to some three reasons "pro" I strike out the five: and thus proceeding, I find at length, where the balance lies: and if, after a day or two of further consideration, nothing new that is of importance occurs on either side, I come to a determination accordingly.

And, though the weight of reasons cannot be taken with algebraic quantities, yet, when each is thus considered separately and comparatively, and the whole lies before me, I think I can judge better, and am less liable to make a rash step; in fact, I have found great advantage from this kind of equation in what may be called *moral or prudential algebra.*

Wishing sincerely that you may determine for the best, I am ever, my dear friend,

Yours most affectionately,
Benjamin Franklin

Let us apply Franklin's Moral Algebra to screen two skeletal solutions to the Parking Space Assignment problem. Use your one-page executive summaries to identify the pros and cons. The team's discussion also provides an additional source of pro and con arguments.

Idea 1: Assign spaces to sharpest, or most productive, workers.

Pros	Cons
1. Improve morale of workers.	1. Could create a too competitive environment.
2. Improve plant productivity.	2. Management team might resent loss of parking perk.
3. Management team treated equally.	

Idea 2: Ask for change in present company policy on need for visitor parking spaces.

Pros	*Cons*
1. Management team treated equally.	1. Unlikely to be approved.
	2. May make it difficult to approach senior management on more important matters.
	3. May alienate the workers who have to park across the street.
	4. May alienate visitors who have to park across the street.

Now evaluate the pros and cons. For Idea 1, the team equated the two con arguments to one of the pro arguments. Thus the idea has a prudential algebra score of +2. For Idea 2, the team equated the one pro argument to two of the con arguments. Thus Idea 2 has a prudential algebra score of –2. In this fashion the team decided which skeletal ideas to pursue. Consider screening when your team develops more than three skeletal ideas.

SUMMARY

Diagnosis and alternative generation are the most critical activities in problem solving. In diagnosing disturbance problems you seek causes using the K-T or Alternative Worldview methods. If you know the causes but still have not solved the problem, consider goal reformulation.

In diagnosing entrepreneurial problems, consider goal reformulation using the Problem Boundary Expansion or the 5Ws methods. This opens new vistas for searching for alternative solutions. A problem cannot be solved unless its causes are known or its goals clearly articulated.

In developing alternatives, generate six to ten skeletal ideas using the Nominal Group Technique or the Analogy Method. Then, using either the nominal group voting procedure or moral algebra, you screen the list and narrow it down to the two or three best ideas.

You then flesh out the best ideas. Do your homework and collect supporting data. Find out what the final authorizers demand for an acceptable proposal. What quantitative and qualitative data do they want to see? What format do they prefer? Do they want a summary first followed by the details, or the details first followed by a summary? Of course, the final packaging can be postponed until you have made your choice. But you need to start thinking about it as you flesh out the final two or three ideas.

You are now well on your way to producing good apples.

ENDNOTES

1. William F. Pounds, "The Process of Problem Finding," *Industrial Management Review* (Fall 1969): 1–19.

2. W. Abernathy and R. Rosenbloom, "Parallel Strategies in Developmental Projects," *Management Science* 15, no. 10 (1969): 486–505; Irving Janis and Leon Mann, *Decision Making: A Psychological Analysis of Conflict, Choice, and Commitment* (New York: Free Press, 1977).

3. Peter F. Drucker, "What We Can Learn from Japanese Management," *Harvard Business Review* (March-April 1971): 110–22.

4. Henry Mintzberg, Duru Raisinghani, and Andre Theoret, "The Structure of Unstructured Decision Processes," *Administrative Science Quarterly* (June 1976): 246–75.

5. Carolyne Smart and Ilan Vertinsky, "Designs for Crisis Decision Units," *Administrative Science Quarterly* (December 1977): 640–57.

6. Peter Drucker, "What We Can Learn," 110–22.

7. Marjorie Lyles and Ian Mitroff, "Organizational Problem Formulation: An Empirical Study," *Administrative Science Quarterly* (March 1980): 102–19.

8. Karen Brown, "Explaining Group Poor Performance: An Attributional Analysis," *Academy of Management Review* 9, no. 1 (1984): 54–63.

9. H. Kelley and J. Michael, "Attribution Theory and Research," in M. Rosenzweig and L. Porter (eds.), *Annual Review of Psychology* (Palo Alto, California: Annual Reviews Inc., 1980), 457–501.

10. H. Weiss and J. Shaw, "Social Influences on Judgments about Tasks," *Organizational Behavior and Human Performance* 24 (1979): 126–40.

11. T. Mitchell and I. Kalb, "The Effects of Job Experience on Supervisory Attribution for a Subordinate's Poor Performance," *Journal of Applied Psychology* 67 (1982): 181–88.

12. Lyles and Mitroff, "Organizational Problem Formulation," 102–19.

13. Ibid., 112.

14. Ibid., 115.

15. Paul Nutt, "Types of Organizational Decision Processes," *Administrative Science Quarterly* (September 1984): 414–50; Mintzberg, Raisinghani, and Theoret, "Unstructured Decision Processes," 246–75.

16. Ernest Alexander, "The Design of Alternatives in Organizational Contexts," *Administrative Science Quarterly* (September 1979): 382–404.

17. Harvey Brightman, "The Structure of the Unstructured Acquisition Decision." (Paper presented at the annual meeting of the Decision Sciences Institute, Las Vegas, Nevada, November 1985.)

18. Nutt, "Types of Organizational Decision Processes," 433.

19. Charles Kepner and Benjamin Tregoe, *The Rational Manager* (New York: McGraw-Hill, 1965) 20–25.

20. P. Stryker, "Can You Analyze This Problem," *Harvard Business Review* (May-June 1965): 73–78.

21. C. West Churchman, *The Design of Inquiring Systems* (New York: Basic Books, 1971), 171.

22. *Wall Street Journal*, 22 October 1975.

23. Edward Hodnett, *The Art of Problem Solving* (New York: Harper and Row, 1955), 109.

24. Rodger Vokema, "Problem Formulation in Planning and Design," *Management Science* 29, no. 6 (1983): 639-52.

25. Victor Vroom and Arthur Yago, "Decision Making as a Social Process: Normative and Descriptive Models of Leader Behavior," *Decision Sciences* (October 1974): 743-69.

26. Arthur VanGundy, *Managing Group Creativity* (New York: AMACOM, 1984): 156-57.

IMPROVING
DECISION
MAKING
and
IMPLEMENTATION

You have learned to diagnose problems and to generate several detailed alternative solutions. Now we focus on several rigorous strategies for selecting the best action and implementing it. Our goal is to take the good apples we produced in Chapter 5 and bake good apple pies.

PROBLEMS IN REAL-WORLD PRACTICE

Decision Making: An Implicit Process

Decision making is not a formal competition among competing ideas to accomplish a set of goals. It is not an organized activity. Rather, it resembles the games we played as youngsters. Often the teams changed from game to game and the rules were flexible. Likewise, in decision making managers often do not identify goals or formally evaluate alternatives. Sometimes we cannot even pinpoint when a decision has been made.

Often managers do not explicitly set decision goals. Rather, they create them after they have chosen an action. The goals serve to *rationalize* the decision.[1] For example, a CEO wanted to buy a prestigious sports franchise. To create a need for action, he helped his board of directors uncover a hitherto unknown critical problem. Then he fashioned his decision goals, based on what his pet solution could deliver. The CEO then demonstrated how the franchise would solve the problem. To the board, the sports franchise must have seemed like a match made in heaven.[2]

That is not all. Managers often do not formally evaluate options. In the sports franchise decision, the CEO assembled voluminous financial data. But he had decided to purchase when he first heard that the franchise was available. So what was the purpose of the financial data? It was to placate the lending institutions, which were important stakeholders to his firm.

Often alternatives simply die without their "day in court." Administrative theorist Ernest Alexander illustrates this in his discussion of our Vietnam policy:

> In some cases, alternatives were eliminated almost intuitively, applying informal selection criteria. . . . For example, in the evolution of Vietnam policy, non-escalation alternatives were dismissed without formal evaluation by the rigid application of the "domino theory," the dominant ideological paradigm in the U.S. policy establishment.[3]

Frequently we cannot even identify when a decision is made. It just happens. Marion Folson, a top executive in business, said it this way:

> It is often hard to pinpoint the exact stage at which a decision is reached. More often than not the decision comes about naturally during the discussions, when the consensus seems to be reached among those whose judgment and opinion the executive seeks.[4]

Decision Making: Beyond Analysis

Managers use analytical choice-making strategies less than 10% of the time.[5] They may not be aware of simple, yet powerful, analytical techniques. Or managers may mistakenly consider them too pedantic. Finally, for some entrepreneurial problems it may be difficult to identify goals and outcomes. Thus, choice making transcends analysis. It is a judgmental process. Unfortunately, risk aversion, political factors, and compromise strategies invade the process.

Managers minimize risk by bypassing formal evaluation and doing what others have done. They choose solutions that have already been successfully used elsewhere. We call this *demonstrated workability*. This strategy has its advantages. It helps sell a solution to the ultimate authorizers. And if the solution does not work, the team cannot be faulted. After all, the solution has worked for other firms. CEOs are pragmatic, and perhaps that is why they rely on demonstrated workability. Moreover, too many managers believe that failures have greater impact on their careers than innovative ideas that work.[6] The message: Successes are fleeting, but failures endure.

Risk-aversion strategies can be ineffective. Remember, all problems are not alike. Avoid the "Peter Principle" in using others' solutions. Only identical problems call for identical solutions. Develop innovative solutions and formally evaluate them. Risk-averting managers or CEOs see only the potential downside consequences. Where are the visionary leaders such as Walt Disney or Ray Kroc? A nation of risk averters is a nation at risk.

Often options are not evaluated on their own merits. As in problem diagnosis, the sponsor's political clout is a critical factor. Political factors clearly influenced President Truman's seizure of the steel mills during the Korean War.[7]

In 1950 President Truman established the Office of Price Stabilization (OPS) and the Wage Stabilization Board (WSB). The OPS developed guidelines for evaluating price increases, and the WSB developed guidelines for reviewing wage-hike requests in the steel industry. Both groups reported to Charles Wilson. Ellis Arnall, a close personal friend of Truman, headed OPS.

In late March 1952 the WSB announced its wage-hike recommendations. Wilson thought that they were too high, but conferred with steel industry leaders. He asked Arnall to relax the OPS guidelines to allow the steel companies to pass on the wage hikes to their customers. Wilson thought this would avert an industry lockout and keep critical war material flowing. Arnall would have none of it. Claiming to be working under a mandate from the president, Wilson fought for a $5.50 per ton price increase. Again Arnall was adamant. He insisted on hearing it from the president. In a showdown, the president sided with Arnall. Although Wilson was Arnall's superior, Arnall had more political clout. The steel companies rejected the OPS recommendation, and Truman was forced to seize the mills. Political factors play a significant role in diagnosing problems and evaluating options. The best options do not always win.

Compromise is a critical element in choice making, especially in the public sector. Here, opposing team members try to influence the decision. Sometimes the solution is not objectively the best but will be acceptable to all parties. Thus it stands a greater chance of actually being implemented. The effectiveness of the MARTA Committee of 50 (Chapter 4) clearly illustrates this strategy.

Implementing Solutions: The Missing Link

As Yogi Berra used to say: "It ain't over till it's over." Until you have successfully installed your solution, you have not accomplished anything. Too often, we forget this simple premise. We naively assume that our colleagues will support good solutions. But when a solution is either innovative or calls for a realignment of power or resources, installation may not be smooth. Yes, Virginia, there are people out there who want to see you fail. We call them *counter-implementors*. They rely on inertia to stop a project. They may try to embellish your solution. They know that complex solutions are more difficult to coordinate and take longer to install because key implementation personnel are more likely to leave or be transferred. Finally, counter-implementors may try to minimize your legitimacy and influence or play counter-implementation games. In short, they play "hard ball." We must do likewise.

Implementation cannot be an afterthought. Do not wait until your solution has been authorized to begin thinking about it. Begin with team membership. Ask the installers to join your problem-solving team. Raise implementation issues during alternative generation As you flesh out the final contenders, include a brief installation plan. After a solution has been authorized, then you can develop a detailed plan. Implementation must be an essential thread throughout your decision-making process.

GENERAL PRINCIPLES IN DECISION MAKING

There are serious problems in real-world practice. Decision making is often an implicit process. Moreover, managers carry excess baggage. They may choose mediocre solutions because they are risk averters or factor in political considerations. In proposing choice-making procedures, I am guided by the principles that follow.

PRINCIPLE 1: *The choice procedure should be rigorous but not complex or mathematical.*

No one uses complex procedures they do not understand. The procedures should guide your team through choice making. It should be rational and expeditious. It should help your team avoid the biases discussed in Chapter 2. Finally, it should help you explain your decision to the authorizers.

PRINCIPLE 2: *Don't start formally evaluating your alternative options until they are fleshed out.*

While diagnosis and alternative generation must be interconnected, choice making must be a distinct activity. Alternative actions flow from your definition of a problem. Imagine that your team's goal is to reduce car accidents. Using the 5Ws Method (Chapter 5), team members develop three problem definitions. Note how each definition suggests different alternative solutions:
- In what ways might we remove unsafe drivers from the road?
- In what ways might we upgrade car safety standards?
- In what ways might we improve roadways?

However, alternative generation and formal choice making must be distinct activities. Only evaluate solutions during screening or during formal choice making. Otherwise you can reject an idea before you understand it or have most of the evaluative data. We call this premature closure.

PRINCIPLE 3: *Even if you make the final decision yourself, have your team members participate.*

A team can serve two purposes. *Information-sharing* teams generate and share information. *Participative problem-solving* teams are empowered to make the final decision. In both cases, members' participation is essential. If you have formed a team, do not disband it before completing the choice and implementation activities.

FORMAL METHODS FOR MAKING CHOICES

MATRIX WEIGHTING	CRITICAL/CONVERGENT
ASSUMPTION SURFACING	CRITICAL/CONVERGENT

You begin the Matrix-weighting Method by assigning weights to your decision goals.[8] Then you assess how well the options accomplish each goal. Finally you compute a *figure of merit* (FOM) score that allows you to compare your options. Select the option that best achieves your goals. Use this approach when choosing among a very large number of possible alternatives.

The Assumption-surfacing Method is especially effective when evaluating only two or three options.[9] Begin by assuming that your first option best accomplishes each goal. What assumptions must be true about various stakeholders if the first option is really the best solution? Now repeat the process for the other options. Select that option with the most reasonable set of underlying assumptions.

The Matrix-weighting Method

1. Construct a scoring matrix as shown in Exhibit 6-1.

Along the top row are the decision goals that you developed during problem formulation or that surfaced during alternative screening. Along the left side of the matrix are your options.

2. Have the team assign *objective scores* and *relative weights* for all goals.

First assign objective scores. The most important objective has a score of 100. Place the remaining goals on the following scale to reflect their importance in comparison to the most important goal.

Determine the relative weight of a goal by computing its objective score divided by the objective score for the least important objective.

Using this procedure, have each member independently develop their own objective scores and relative weights for all decision goals. Now use the Nominal Group Technique to reconcile any differences.

3. Assign *evaluation scores.* Evaluate option 1 on all the decision goals.

If you believe that an option fully accomplishes a goal, assign it a score of 10. If an alternative totally fails to meet a goal, assign it a score of 1.

Have each member independently evaluate the first option on all the decision goals. Again use the Nominal Group Technique to reach a consensus.

4. Repeat step 3 for all options.

5. Compute an FOM score. For each option, multiply the evaluation scores by their respective relative weights and sum them.

6. The option with the highest FOM score has the strongest support.

EXHIBIT 6-1
Example of a Scoring Matrix

	Decision Goals and Relative Weights			
Alternatives	Goal 1 [1*]	Goal 2 [1]	Goal 3 [2]	FOM score
Option 1	7	5	3	18
Option 2	5	5	10	30
Option 3	3	6	7	23
Option 4	3	1	8	20

* Relative weight for the first goal.

Let's apply the Matrix-weighting Method to the following disturbance problem.

The Case of the Dying Institute. A firm's senior management wanted additional training for its middle managers. The human resources group conducted a needs assessment and hired a faculty team to help develop a curriculum of eight courses, each lasting about 12 to 16 hours. The courses were offered during the workweek, and managers were given time off to attend.

Senior management heavily promoted the institute. The program and its objectives were well-communicated to the participants. Representatives of the faculty, senior management, and future participants held joint meetings to discuss the goals of the institute. There was much initial enthusiasm.

In the first year, an average of 25 individuals registered for each course—about what senior management had expected. However, only 8 to 10 people actually attended the sessions. This happened for all courses. Attendees agreed that the training was effective and relevant to their on-the-job needs.

The CEO told his middle managers that he was dissatisfied with their attendance. He reiterated the importance of the institute to the long-term goals of the company. Everyone thought that attendance would increase. Unfortunately the problem reoccurred in the second year—for each course, 25 managers preregistered, but only 10 attended.

Unless something could be done, the program would be canceled. The CEO formed a team of faculty, graduates, and resource group personnel. Let's retrace the team's steps in solving this problem.

The team began with the following initial decision goal: We want *to increase attendance to 25 managers.*

Using Problem Boundary Expansion (Chapter 5), the team generated ten additional potential decision goals. They agreed to the following three goals:

Attendance — Increase attendance to 25 managers per course.

Application — Make maximum use of the techniques learned in the courses back on the job.

Renewal — Have participants grow as professional managers and keep abreast of the latest methods after completing the program.

Using Analogy (Chapter 5), the team developed over 60 skeletal solutions. After screening, the following four solutions were fleshed out:

Alumni Club — Form a club of managers who have completed the institute. The club would (1) remind, cajole, and help managers attend the institute; (2) help redesign the institute's objectives and courses; (3) form an in-house, end-user's group to help alumni use the techniques and learn new ones.

Promotion — Make completion of the institute a prerequisite for promotion. The military uses this strategy. To obtain a senior rank, an officer must graduate from a War College.

Big Stick — Managers must attend the courses or have an excused absence. All unexcused absences must be explained to the division head or CEO in person.

Yearly Review — Incorporate into the annual review a requirement that participants provide evidence of what techniques they have used on the job.

Using the Nominal Group Technique, the team agreed on the following objective scores and relative weights.

Decision goals	Objective scores	Relative weights
Attendance	80	80/40 = 2.0
Application	100	100/40 = 2.5
Renewal	40	40/40 = 1.0

The team members, silently and independently, evaluated each option for the three decision goals. They assigned evaluations scores from 1 (totally failed to accomplish goal) to 10. The team used the Nominal Group Technique to resolve any evaluation differences. Exhibit 6-2 contains the analysis of the four options.

EXHIBIT 6-2
A Scoring Matrix for the Dying Institute Problem

	Decision Goals and Relative Weights			
Options	Attendance [2.0]	Application [2.5]	Renewal [1]	FOM score
Alumni club	6	8	10	42
Promotion	10	4	3	33
Big stick	9	3	3	28.5
Yearly review	10	10	3	48

The alumni club and yearly review options are the best. Which should the team implement? The option with the fewest implementation problems based on a potential problem analysis.

Assumption-surfacing Method

An option is best only if its underlying assumptions are true. Assumptions underlie all alternatives. Unfortunately, we often do not share our assumptions with others. Sometimes we are not even aware of what they are, so we cannot subject them to public scrutiny.

Researcher James O'Toole shows how a set of ten basic assumptions guided the success of General Motors (GM) during its first 50 years.[10] It also guided their decline through the turbulent seventies. GM never explicitly challenged these assumptions until the late seventies:

1. GM is in the business of making money, not cars.
2. Success does not come from technological leadership. It rests on the ability to adopt innovation quickly.
3. Cars are status symbols. Styling is the critical factor in the consumer purchasing decision.
4. The American car market is isolated from foreign competition.
5. Energy is cheap and abundant.
6. Workers do not have an important impact on product quality or productivity.
7. The consumer movement is weak.
8. The government is the enemy.
9. Strict centralized financial controls are critical to success.
10. Managers must be developed outside.

In the seventies these assumptions were wrong. Gasoline became expensive. The automobile market became internationalized and only technological leadership could contain skyrocketing tooling costs. Buyers began to read *Consumer Reports*. Consumers wanted quality, and could not afford to purchase cars every two to three years. In short, the assumptions underlying the first 50 years of GM's existence were no longer valid. Thus, GM's actions and policies became invalid. And the marketplace dramatically shared this information with GM.

Assumption surfacing sheds light on our assumptions and helps us select the best option. Here is how it works.

1. *Form Subgroups:* Subdivide your team into subgroups. Assign each option to a subgroup. Alternatively, have team members form subgroups and choose the option they wish to defend or examine.

2. *Generate Stakeholders:* Solutions have impacts on many stakeholders. Managers often implicitly and incorrectly assume what various stakeholders want, believe, expect, or value. The five ways to generate stakeholders are the power, fishnet, other side, informal leader, and silent majority approaches (Chapter 4).

Each subgroup lists all the potential stakeholders who may affect or be affected by their option. Subgroup members, silently and independently, identify stakeholders. Using the Nominal Group Technique they reach a consensus.

3. *Surface Assumptions:* Now the subgroup determines what assumptions must be true about various stakeholders for their option to be best. Do not worry at this stage whether the assumptions are true or false. You will soon evaluate them. Subgroup members, silently and independently, generate assumptions about each stakeholder. Using the Nominal Group Technique they reach a consensus.

4. *Classify Assumptions:* Assumptions fall into one of the following four categories:

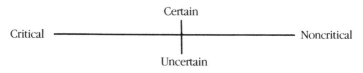

Some assumptions are more important than others. A critical assumption is one that, if false, undermines your option. A fact is an assumption that has a high degree of certainty— perhaps 100%.

Only critical assumptions need be considered further. The uncertain critical assumptions (southwest quadrant) are your option's Achilles' heel. They are critical but you do not know whether they are true. Your subgroup must seek more data to remove their uncertainty.

Each subgroup classifies its assumptions among the four categories just illustrated. Members, silently and independently, classify their subgroup's assumptions. Using the Nominal Group Technique they reach a consensus.

5. *Debate Assumptions:* Call a plenary session. Have each subgroup present their best evidence in support of their option. Now the team *as a whole* debates all the evidence using the Nominal Group Technique. Be prepared to modify or discard your assumptions.

6. *Reach Agreement:* The team *as a whole* develops a final list of reasonable assumptions. They then have two choices:
• Select the best option—the one with the most reasonable assumptions.
• Incorporate the new assumptions during the debate and modify the best option.

Imagine that a team has been formed to use the Assumption-surfacing Method to evaluate the Alumni Club and Yearly Review options. The team is divided into subgroups, and each selects one of the options. Let's follow their deliberations.

Generate Stakeholders. Below are the two stakeholder lists. Each was developed using the Nominal Group Technique.

Stakeholders for the Alumni Club Option	*Stakeholders for the Yearly Review Option*
Alumni (previous participants)	Future participants
Future participants	Faculty
Faculty	Human resources group
Human resources group	Senior management
Senior management	Participants' superiors
	Participants' subordinates

Some stakeholders appear on only one list. For example, the participants' superiors play an important part in the yearly review. They conduct the review. Moreover, if they are to consider the techniques in the evaluation, they must provide time for the participants to practice these techniques on the job. Alumni are important stakeholders only for the alumni club option. They have an important role to play if the club is to be successful.

Surface assumptions. To surface the assumptions behind each option, each subgroup asks the "what must be true" question: In order for my option to be best in accomplishing the attendance goal (or application or renewal goals), what must we *assume* is *true* for each stakeholder?

Each subgroup member, silently and independently, applied the "what must be true" question to each stakeholder. Exhibits

6-3 and 6-4 contain the consensus assumptions underlying the Alumni Club and Yearly Review options.

Classify Assumptions. Which assumptions are critical? Is there any doubt regarding the truth of the assumptions? The goal is to identify the critical assumptions. Exhibit 6-5 shows how one member classified her subgroup's assumptions.

She was uncertain about 9 of the 11 critical assumptions. Of these, she was most uncertain about the cluster of 5 in the extreme southwestern quadrant (R-3, APP-3, R-1, R-2, APP-1). If the other subgroup members agree with her classification, they must seek data to reduce their uncertainty and get at the truth. If there is significant disagreement between members' classifications, consider using the Rational Argumentation Model (Chapter 3):

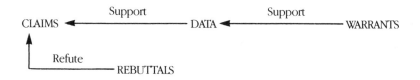

Each assumption is a claim. Now you must present supporting data. Who or what says that your claim is correct? Why should I believe you? Where is the evidence? The warrants tell us why other team members should accept your data as support for the claim. So you presented this data—so what! As we have learned, warrants are rules, principles, and premises that act as a bridge between the data and the claim. The rebuttal provides a safety valve for the argument. It states the conditions under which the claim may not be true. It helps to qualify and assess the claim's plausibility.

Let's apply the Rational Argumentation Model to the APP-1 assumption. As Exhibit 6-5 indicates, it is the most uncertain, yet critical, assumption underlying the Alumni Club option.

Claim: Alumni members will be effective in getting their colleagues to use techniques.

Given: The techniques have not been used because participants need additional on-the-job support. However, the techniques are right on target. This is based on recent interviews with participants who have and have not used the techniques. The difference is the degree of support they have received.

Because: The data are valid because the interviews were conducted properly. Anonymity was insured.

Unless: The sample size was too small to draw any valid conclusions.

Conclusion: Interview more alumni and see if they agree with original survey results. If so we are certain of the assumption's validity. We can use it in the structured debate that follows.

Debate and Reach Consensus. Let us suppose that each subgroup has identified its critical assumptions. Now both subgroups engage in a structured debate during a plenary session. Using the Nominal Group Technique, they present their assumptions and supporting data. The two groups can now evaluate each others' assumptions and data. Their goal is to reach a consensus on a final list of assumptions. They can then either accept one option or modify the best option to incorporate new or modified assumptions.

Comparing the Two Choice Methods

The Matrix-weighting and Assumption-surfacing methods are both analytical techniques. But, as Exhibit 6-6 shows, they have some differences.

Your only goal in matrix-weighting is to select the best option. Assumption-surfacing does this, but it does more. You can use it to modify the best option to make it better. During the debate you may discover that even the best option has some hidden weaknesses. There is still time to redesign it.

Assumption-surfacing is the more versatile method. But you pay a price. Team members can find it more difficult to use. Subgroup members must learn how to argue strongly for their
(Text continued on page 192)

EXHIBIT 6-3
Assumptions Developed by the Subgroup Analyzing the Alumni Club Option

On the attendance objective	On the application objective	On the renewal objective
1. Alumni can be more effective than Human Resource Group personnel in getting managers to workshops.	1. Alumni members will be effective in getting their colleagues to use techniques. The techniques are appropriate. However, potential end-users need a support group.	1. Alumni want and are capable of assuming responsibility for the club in addition to their busy schedules.
2. Future participants will listen to colleagues and will attend. The busy calendar and the need to deal with crisis problems have kept attendance down. Colleagues can assure participants that they will be able to attend the courses and deal with the crises.	2. Alumni members are qualified to design or modify the curriculum.	2. Alumni want self-renewal, and a group is more effective than doing it alone.
3. The faculty will reenforce the alumni's mission of "getting out the troops."	3. Future participants will use techniques if supported by colleagues. Lack of support has caused alumni not to use techniques.	3. Future participants will want to join an alumni club. Otherwise the entire burden falls on the shoulders of the founders.

4. The Human Resource Group will view the club as a positive force in getting people to the courses. They will suffer no loss of face.

5. Club members will have access to senior management.

4. The faculty is willing to implement or seriously consider inputs from club members on workshop content.

5. The Human Resource Group is willing to implement or seriously consider inputs from club members on workshop content.

6. Senior management will reward those who use the techniques on the job.

4. Faculty will provide input into the alumni club and suggest periodicals, books, and so forth.

5. The Human Resource Group will support an alumni club which ex-cludes training personnel.

6. Senior management will provide support to hold meetings, purchase periodicals and books, and sponsor "booster" programs when needed.

7. Senior management will give formal recognition to the alumni group as an important organizational resource.

EXHIBIT 6-4

Assumptions Developed by the Subgroup Analyzing the Yearly Review Option

On the attendance objective	On the application objective	On the renewal objective
1. Future participants are externally motivated by the reward system.	1. Future participants are externally motivated by the reward system.	1. Future participants will internalize the goals of the Institute.
2. Faculty has developed a program that is equally applicable to all managers.	2. Faculty will not object to becoming a part of the formal evaluation system. They have no fear that their neutrality will be compromised.	2. Future alumni want self-renewal and it can best be done alone.
3. The Human Resources Group must be able to continue their consulting services to the firm. Their indirect involvement in the financial reward system must not compromise their other services.	3. Faculty will not subvert the program to meet managers' present needs at the expense of future requirements.	3. Faculty can motivate participants to continue the learning process started in the Institute.

4. Senior management will not over-rule a poor evaluation of an otherwise exceptional performer merely because he or she has not used the techniques they have learned in the workshop.

5. Participants' superiors will not complain when managers attend the courses. They will allow attendees more time to complete their required assignments.

6. Participants' subordinates are willing to cover for their superiors during the workshop.

4. Senior management can develop an evaluation system for measuring managers' use of techniques.

5. Participants' superors will allow them to try new techniques on the job. Superiors will allow for the learning curve.

6. As most problem solving within the firm is done in teams, participants' subordinates will want and are capable of learning the techniques.

4. Faculty has given attendees the necessary skills to read the literature and learn on their own.

5. Senior management will include a section in the yearly review that focuses on evidence of renewal and individual growth.

6. Participants' superiors will also adopt some of the new techniques and thus provide a positive example of self-renewal.

EXHIBIT 6-5
**A Member's Classification of the Assumptions
Underlying the Alumni Club Option**

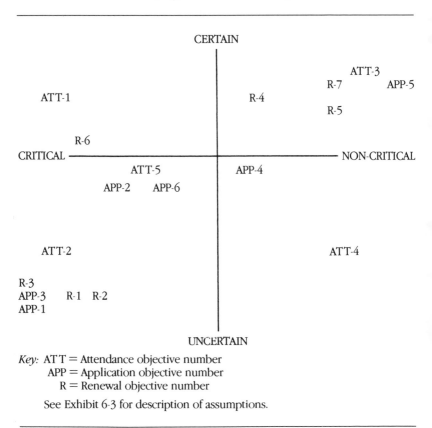

Key: ATT = Attendance objective number
APP = Application objective number
R = Renewal objective number

See Exhibit 6-3 for description of assumptions.

(Text continued from page 187)

option but not be dogmatic. They must learn that the process of debate and resolution will strengthen whatever option the team selects. Subgroup members may find assumption-surfacing intellectually appealing. Emotionally they may find it appalling. Subgroup members may become emotionally attached to their option. And if it is rejected, they may experience loss of face. Assumption-surfacing is not a contest between subgroups. Rather it is a contest between ideas. But are we capable of divorcing emotion from intellect?

EXHIBIT 6-6
Comparing the Matrix-weighting and Assumption-surfacing Methods

Attribute	Matrix-weighting	Assumption-surfacing
Approach	Assess how well an option accomplishes goals.	Analyze fundamental decision assumptions underlying options.
Goals	Select the best option.	Surface underlying assumptions. Modify a good option and make it better. Select the best option.
Number of options	Examine many options.	Examine two or three options.
Process	Seek a consensus using the Nominal Group Technique.	Debate first, and then seek a consensus using the Nominal Group Technique.
Emotional tone of meetings	Must be willing to modify your position discussing the relative weights and the evaluation scores during the consensus phase.	Must believe in your option. Must try to make the strongest case you can. Must be willing to listen to the other side during the debate. Must be willing to modify your beliefs during the consensus phase. Your motto must be: Fight hard for what you believe in, but don't be dogmatic.
Ease of use	Very easy to use.	More difficult to use.

SECOND-LOOK MEETING

REALITY-TESTING	CRITICAL/CONVERGENT
POTENTIAL PROBLEM ANALYSIS	CREATIVE/DIVERGENT

Once you have made a tentative choice, schedule a second-look meeting. It serves two purposes. First you reconsider those options that were previously rejected during screening or choice. The goal is to reality-test your chosen option. You also seek to uncover potential problems that might arise during implementation. Imagine you are implementing your solution. Assume that Murphy was an optimist. What will go wrong? And how can you overcome these potential problems? Potential Problem Analysis is essential to implementation success.[11]

Reality-testing

You have been working on a problem for several weeks. After much discussion, you've made your final choice. But is it the best solution? Since rejecting earlier options, you may have uncovered significant new information. Could a previously rejected option now be better than your chosen option? Without a second-look meeting you will never know.

Sift through rejected options (include those rejected at screening or earlier). We call them "preemies." Select several of the most promising ones and assign them to team members. Then schedule another meeting several days later. In the interim, ask each member to reexamine his "preemie." Now with all the data, how does it compare to the chosen option? At the team meeting each member then plays devil's advocate to the chosen option. Members try to demonstrate that their "preemie" is superior.

Members should especially focus on the long-term consequences of the options. We know that a solution can create more problems than it solves. The State of Georgia transplanted kudzu (a plant) to control soil erosion. It grew like wildfire and did its job. Unfortunately kudzu is now strangling the forests of Georgia.

It wraps itself around trees and smothers them. Nothing can stop it. Some solution!

Could your option produce future unintended problems? What are they and how likely are they? If the Alumni Club solves the Dying Institute problem, will middle management ask for increasing levels of participation in areas beyond the institute? And is senior management prepared to respond positively? If the Yearly Review works, will institute graduates require a similar review for their subordinates? And if they do, who will train them? The institute may not be equipped to handle the numbers, and the graduates may not have time to train their own subordinates. Thus subordinates' evaluations will be partially based on using techniques that no one has time to teach them.

Second-look meetings produce one of two outcomes. A "preemie" may turn out to be better than the chosen option. If so, discard your original option. Replace it with a fully designed version of the "preemie." If all the "preemies" are rejected, that too is good. For now you can, with greater confidence, tell the ultimate authorizers that you selected the best option. It has met every challenge.

Potential Problem Analysis

Imagine that your option has been approved. You are ready to install it. Potential Problem Analysis will help determine what could go wrong during the installation:

1. Use the 5Ws Method or the Gamesmanship Model to develop a list of potential installation problems.[12]

2. Using a 10-point scale, assess the chances of each problem happening and its potential seriousness:

Likelihood: A score of 10 means that the problem is very likely to happen. A score of 1 means that the problem is very unlikely to happen.

Seriousness: A score of 10 means that the problem will seriously impede installation. A score of 1 means that the problem has a trivial effect on the installation.

3. Multiply each likelihood number by its seriousness value. This is the expected-trouble quotient. As it increases, so do your implementation problems.

4. Develop countermeasures for any potential problem that you consider has a high expected-trouble quotient.

We first discussed the 5Ws Method as a goal reformulation tool (Chapter 5). You can also apply it to identify potential installation problems. Ask who, what, where, when, and why before installing your solution. The first four pronouns identify potential problems. "Why" helps us determine what can be done to overcome the problem. It is the beginning of counter counter-implementation tactics.

Who will install the solution? Why should they strive to do their best? Who will oppose it? Why are they in opposition? What internal, external, human, or technological problems are we likely to encounter? Why will we encounter them? What are the critical components in the installation? Why are they critical? Where will we face the greatest coordination problems? Why are the coordination problems acute? When must each step of the installation be completed? Why can't we reschedule the steps to reduce potential problems?

Is your solution controversial? Is it innovative and will it require new on-the-job behaviors? Do you anticipate political problems in installing your solution? If so, consider using the Gamesmanship Model to generate potential problems. According to political scientist Eugene Bardach, installing a solution often requires the cooperation of many groups. But all groups may not be sold on your solution. This leads to territorial disputes, maneuvering for position, conflict over goals, and irreconcilable differences in perspective. We call those who wish to block our installation counter-implementors (CIs). They lay low, rely on inertia, and play "games" to stop us. Some of the games are described in Exhibit 6-7. Counter-implementors play dirty games. We must be ready to respond. One way to beat them is scenario writing and networking.

What problems might arise in installing the Alumni Club option? How likely are they, and could they quash an installation? The results are shown in Exhibit 6-8. We identified

(Text continued on page 200)

EXHIBIT 6-7
Games that Counter-implementors Play

Major tactic	Games	How it works
Deflect goals	Piling on	Kill an option with kindness. Counter-implementors suggest increasing the option's scope and complexity. They know that more complex projects are more difficult to install.
	The fifth column	Counter-implementors join the implementation team as a peace-keeping gesture. Their real goal is to promote chaos, delay, and inertia.
Divert resources	Easy life	"Let's take this project slowly." "Let's make this project as easy on everyone as possible." The counter-implementors' real goal is massive delay.
	Play money	Inflate the dollar or man-hour estimates needed to install your option. Can cause delay or outright reevaluation of the option.

(Continued on next page)

Dissipate energy	We'll do it our way	Counter-implementors "support" the option but want to either be in charge or have control of the installation project. Their real goal is massive delay or reevaluation.
	Not our job	Counter-implementors "agree" to the option. But they believe it is outside the scope of their department—"We'd like to help install the option but that is not our job."
	Odd man out	Counter-implementors tell you they support the option. But they won't commit their resources until other groups jump on board. If many groups feel this way, the project will die.

EXHIBIT 6-8
Potential Problem Analysis for the Alumni Club Option

Potential problem	Seriousness [2]	Likelihood [3]	Expected trouble quotient [2] × [3]
1. Strongest alumni supporters transferred during formation of the club.	10	1	10
2. Group loses interest in total mission. Becomes a social club.	8	4	32
3. Cannot find an effective part-time (unpaid) club director.	6	8	48
4. Club underfinanced at inception.	10	4	40
5. Piling on—Human Resources Group increases the scope of club.	8	5	40
6. Do it our way—Faculty want control over club.	6	1	6
7. Keep peace—Human Resources Group joins effort but will undermine the club during formation.	10	3	30

(Text continued from page 196)
the first four problems using the 5Ws Method and the last three problems using the Gamesmanship Model. Problems 1 to 4 reflect the vagaries of corporate life. People are transferred. They lose interest in projects over time. Sometimes it is difficult to fill a position. Problems 5 to 7 reflect the politics of implementation. The actions taken by the counter-implementors are premeditated. They want to stop our installation.

The team identified seven potential problems. However, only five (numbers 2 to 5, and 7) are potentially fatal. For these they should develop *formal* countermeasures or contingency plans. These should be part of their overall implementation plans.

IMPLEMENTATION

GANTT CHART	CRITICAL/CONVERGENT
SCENARIO WRITING	CRITICAL/CONVERGENT

After your option has been approved, install it. Installation and implementation are not synonymous. Although installation is a critical part of implementation, there is more to implementation. It actually begins during problem solving. Implementation thinking helps you design options that can easily be installed and that accomplish the desired goals without generating any harmful side effects. It helps ensure that the option is enthusiastically adopted by those it is intended to help. Installing the option is important. But setting the stage for the installation is just as critical.

Remember, sometimes a solution creates worse problems. Harmful side effects often occur, especially in implementing complex solutions. Moreover, to be a complete success, you must sell the option to the problem havers. And they must willingly accept ownership. Otherwise the option will always remain the problem-solving team's solution (also known as "their" solution, not "ours"). To summarize, a successful implementation occurs when: An option accomplishes its short-run goals and does not create worse problems. Most important, the problem havers take ownership of the option.

Why Implementations Fail

First, and most obvious, are design flaws in the solution. It is either ineffective or the decision goals are in conflict with one another. The option simply cannot meet all the goals. Poor management of the implementation process also produces failures. The option could be effective but the team fails to create a need for the solution or botches the installation. Alternatively, when the decision causes major changes in the organization, political factors become critical. Counter-implementors will try to thwart the implementation effort.

Design Flaws. The Model Cities program created by the federal government in 1966 illustrates how design flaws can cripple an option.[13] Congress created the program to accomplish the following goals:

1. Help inner city residents with a variety of services.

2. Strengthen the authority of mayors over social program decision making in their cities.

3. Bring efficiency and economy to a whole set of preexisting overlapping programs.

4. Strengthen local neighborhood leaders by encouraging self-sufficiency, including providing training that would lead them to challenge mayors and city officials efficiently.

How could the Model Cities program be successful when goals 2 and 4 clash head-on? It is not possible to strengthen the authority of mayors while teaching neighborhood leaders to successfully negotiate with city officials. The program was flawed from the start.

Another common design flaw is lack of specificity. The team may never fully detail the chosen option. Thus, no one is sure exactly what the option is. You know that lack of specificity has happened when during installation a team member says, "But I thought our solution . . ." Here we have a disaster waiting to happen.

Perhaps the most common mistake is ignoring implementation issues when designing options. The team should design options within the capability of those who will have to install it. Do not assume that the installers are brilliant or are firmly entrenched in their jobs. Do not wait until the option has been chosen to start thinking about implementation issues. Let it be said one more time: Implementation issues should be a central thread of the decision-making process.

Poor Management Techniques. Sometimes we even fail with uncontroversial options. The most common reason is ineffective management of the installation process. Many people are involved, but no one is in charge. There are too many Indians and too few chiefs. Furthermore, we have the potential for coordination problems. And these problems are exacerbated when the team has not developed a formal installation game plan that includes routines or procedures.

Politics of Implementation. The chances of failure increase when the level of conflict is high. And this occurs when others believe that the chosen option will produce major shifts in power or resources. We know that counter-implementors try to deflect the decision goals, divert resources, or waylay an unsuspecting problem-solving team. In short, they play counter-implementation games and use their political clout. We have entered the gamesmanship arena.

Other Factors. Senior management must truly support the option. Mere lip service will not do. Real support must provide resources and political clout whenever they are needed to overcome installation obstacles.[14] Another sure way to kill an option is to expect too much of it. When the beneficiaries of an option have unrealistically high expectations, the option may not deliver and may be scrapped.[15] Finally, members of the problem-solving team may not understand the process or dynamics of implementation. You do not just install an option, you need a strategy to guide the entire implementation process.

Lewin and Schein Model

Implementation is a perilous journey. However, the Lewin

and Schein Model provides a road map for successfully negotiating each step of the implementation:[16]

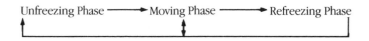

Good Practices in the Unfreezing Stage

In *unfreezing* you set the stage for installing your ultimate solution. Unfreezing begins the first day of your problem-solving effort. Now we know that solutions produce change in an organization. While change is inevitable, everyone resists it. Only wet babies like change. We are creatures of habit. Thus, unfreezing is salesmanship. You may need to sell colleagues or senior management on the need for action, your diagnosis, and whatever option you ultimately design.

In the unfreezing stage you create a perceived need to change the status quo. Change can only occur when all agree that it will be beneficial. If the problem havers are not already on your team, invite them to join. They are important stakeholders and have much insight to offer. Encourage them to play an active role in diagnosing the problem, designing "skeletal" solutions, and selecting the final option. You will design more effective solutions when problem solvers and problem havers respect one another.

Also work on building and maintaining networks of supporters throughout the company. They may be able to help you overcome future counter-implementation games. Networking is time-consuming, but it can pay dividends.

Your goal is to create a receptive environment for whatever solution your team ultimately designs. Make it easy on yourself. Begin by designing effective solutions that you can easily implement. Social scientists Randall Ripley and Grace Franklin argue that the Targeted Jobs Tax Credit designed in late 1978 was so flawed that even a perfect installation could have made no difference.[17] They further argue that some programs are so well designed that even a fumbling bureaucracy cannot derail them. They may not work as smoothly as desired, but the problem havers nevertheless still receive the benefits.

Remember, design solutions that are simple to install. And

do not let others complicate your solutions. They may have ulterior motives.

Also, do not assume that your option will sell itself. Your option may encounter opposition when critical stakeholders have not been involved in making the decision, do not trust the problem-solving team, or are likely to lose power or resources. Here, selling important stakeholders and the problem havers is a critical element of the unfreezing stage. Gaining acceptance for the option is as critical as the option itself. For if it is not accepted, it may not be implemented successfully.

Selling an option has additional benefits. The problem havers, or consumers, can give you insight on how best to proceed. Or they can provide your team with additional resources for the installation. Remember, sold consumers are more likely to support the team's solution.

How should you sell your option? The first principle of salesmanship is sell benefits, not features. The problem havers do not want to know what "bells and whistles" you have designed into a solution, but rather, what benefits your solution will deliver. Do not oversell benefits either. You need to manage their expectations. Unrealistic expectations will kill an option.

Good Practices in the Moving Stage

As you enter this stage, you have already chosen your option; now you must install it. Begin by developing detailed formal plans to guide the installation process. These should decompose the installation into a sequence of steps and procedures. Tailor your plan to your personnel. Don't build a plan only a Rambo could carry out when Charlie Brown will have to do it. Then develop contingency plans for the most critical problems dredged up from your potential problem analysis. The moving stage concludes when the option has been installed.

Managing the installation is essential to success. It begins with developing an detailed plan. One effective way to create a plan is the Gantt, or time task analysis, Chart.[18] To create a Gantt Chart you:

1. List every task in installing the option. Be specific and do not leave out any tasks.

2. Estimate the total amount of time you have to install your option.

3. Estimate the amount of time needed to complete each task. When must you start and complete each task?

4. Compare the time required to complete the tasks to the total time you have available. If the tasks require more time than you have available, you must (1) eliminate tasks, (2) do several of the tasks simultaneously, (3) obtain additional resources to reduce task time, or (4) ask for more time to install the option.

5. Construct a chart showing the relationship between each task and its time estimate. Plot the tasks on the vertical axis and time on the horizontal axis.

6. Use your Gantt Chart to install your option and track its progress. If you fall behind schedule, you must take steps to get back on track.

Let us construct a Gantt Chart for the Alumni Club option. The team identified five tasks that must be accomplished within an eight-week period. First, team members must find alumni who will organize the club. The team estimated that this would take about one and one-half weeks and must begin immediately. Next, the team had to find an executive director. This search should begin during the first week and must be completed by the middle of the third week. The completed Gantt Chart is shown in Exhibit 6-9.

Now you can assign installation team members to each of the tasks. You should also determine the resources it will take (time, money, and so forth) to do each task. Obtain those resources and begin the installation.

Use the Gantt Chart to plan, manage, and track an installation. Post the chart in a conspicuous place where all can follow the team's progress. If you fall behind schedule, call a team meeting. Discuss how you can make up for lost time and what resources will be needed to do so.

In developing your plan, keep in mind the following fundamental premises:

EXHIBIT 6-9
A Gantt Chart for Implementing the Alumni Club Option

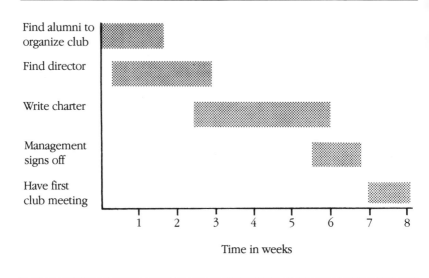

Time in weeks

• Do not build a plan that assumes installers are highly competent. All are not.
• Do not build a plan that assumes installers are highly entrenched in their jobs. People do transfer or quit jobs.

Now you should develop contingency plans for all critical installation problems (Exhibit 6-8). Use the Nominal Group Technique to develop your countermeasures. Each member, silently and independently, develops a plan for each potential problem. A plan includes the countermeasure and a trigger. A trigger is an indicator that tells you when to enact your contingency plan. That is, what data will you need to see before you are convinced that a potential problem is about to occur? This approach works very well for nonpolitical problems (for example, problems 1 through 4, Exhibit 6-8).

When political problems are likely (see problems 5 and 7, Exhibit 6-8), your implementation problems increase. Consider scenario writing in developing your contingency plans.[19] Using the Nominal Group format, ask yourself:

Question: *What resources are needed to overcome the most probable games?*

Team Analysis: We will need to develop countermeasures for "piling on" and "keeping the peace." The essential resource is formal authority to keep the human resources group from playing these games. Unfortunately, our team does not have the necessary authority.

Question: *Who controls the resources, directly or indirectly?*

Team Analysis: The manager of the human resources group is unlikely to stop the games. In fact, he may well be the "ring-leader." The human resources group reports directly to the vice president for administration.

Question: *Will the resource owners cooperate, and if not, how will you work around them or buy them off?*

Team Analysis: At this moment we do not believe that the vice president for administration will intervene if the human resources group plays games. She has more important things to do. How can we get her to intervene on our behalf? Does she owe favors to members of the problem-solving team. Can we speak to her as a colleague and share our concerns?

Question: *Can you redesign your option to thwart the counter-implementors?*

Team Analysis: This should be considered. Perhaps we can remove the human resources group from the game. Our initial option had the club reporting to the manager of the human resources group. Perhaps we can have the club report directly to the vice president for administration? Will senior management accept this? Will the manager of the human resources group accept this?

Question:	*Can you fix the game? Is there a senior person who can help you overcome obstacles? Why should someone fix the game for you?*
Team Analysis:	If the vice president for administration does not intervene, who could stop the human resources group from gameplaying? Perhaps the vice president of marketing will intervene. Although he is not involved with the project, he is your mentor. Perhaps he would be willing to play the fixer role. Consider sharing your concerns with him.
Question:	*Can you build a coalition to fix the game?*
Team Analysis:	Coalitions are unlikely in this company. The firm is similar to sixteenth-century Italy, a country in name only. Each department rules itself and has not wanted to form alliances in the past. But there is always a first time. Perhaps we should consider it if our other approaches fail. Will the networking we did in the unfreezing stage help us forge a coalition?

Clearly, scenario writing will not be necessary for most installations. Often there is no political infighting. But when there is, consider scenario writing. In answering questions such as those proposed, you will be able to minimize the counterimplementors' gameplaying. Remember, the game is not over until you have successfully installed your option.

Good Practices in the Refreezing Stage

A successful implementation requires refreezing. Evaluate whether the option accomplishes the decision goals. Be prepared to modify it if unanticipated negative consequences occur. Refreezing concludes when the problem havers adopt the option and make it their own. The option now loses its separate identity and becomes a part of the organization's ongoing activities. The option has become part of the routine. It has found a home and now belongs to the problem havers. Management information systems' expert Michael Ginzberg tells us that project success is highly related to refreezing success.[20] Do not claim success until you have refrozen the option.

First, determine whether the option obtained the desired goals. You should go beyond the obvious and ask:
• Did the problem havers benefit in additional and unexpected ways? Or did others not intended to benefit also benefit?
• Were the problem havers harmed in some unexpected way? Or were others, inside or outside the department, harmed?
• Were the goals obtained on schedule?

Remember a successful option accomplishes its short-run goals, may generate beneficial unintended consequences, but never creates worse problems.

It is essential that the problem havers buy the solution and make it their own. Sometimes this a most difficult task. A temporary task force or problem-solving team cannot continue to manage the option. When the team disbands, who will direct it? We call this bowing out gracefully, and it must be done. But will the problem havers buy what you are selling? Your chances increase if they have been sold on the idea and have been part of a problem-solving team.

Refreezing closes the problem-solving loop. It comes at the end of a long process. But it should have started when you first found out you had a problem. At every problem-solving step, you and your team should have been thinking: "What must we do to ensure that a successful solution will be a permanent part of the organization's landscape?" When you have refrozen the option, the problem-solving game is over. You've won.

SUMMARY

Decision making is a process or journey. And, in the words of the Neil Diamond song, "the road is long with many a-winding turns." Over the past three chapters we discussed how to outfit yourself for the journey. As we conclude, the Brightman Problem-

EXHIBIT 6-10
A Problem Solver's Guide: Travel Tips and Tourist Traps

Travel tips	*Tourist traps*
Packing the car:	
Form heterogeneous groups.	Mirror, mirror on the wall.
Construct a charter.	We know why we are here, so let's get started.
Find problems.	Don't go looking for problems; they will find you.
On the road:	
Analyze causes.	We have seen this problem before. Why I remember. . . .
Reformulate goals.	The glass is always half-filled.
Generate innovative skeletal ideas.	What have we or others done before?
Screen skeletal ideas.	Clearly there is only one real solution.
At journey's end:	
Explicitly choose an option.	Whose idea was this? I don't remember agreeing to it.
Have a second-look meeting.	Everyone likes our solution. What, me worry?
Design an implementation plan.	Famous last words: Our solution will self-install.

solving Travel Agency offers you these final tips in Exhibit 6-10.

Book your next trip early and avoid the rush. PLAN AHEAD.

ENDNOTES

1. David Braybrooke and Charles Lindblom, *A Strategy of Decision* (New York: Free Press, 1963); E. Eugene Carter, "The Behavioral Theory of the Firm and Top Level Corporate Decisions," *Administrative Science Quarterly* (September 1971): 413–28; Peer Soelberg, "Unprogrammed Decision Making," *Industrial Management Review* (Spring 1967): 19–29.

2. Harvey Brightman, "The Structure of the Unstructured Acquisition Decision," Paper presented at the annual meeting of the Decision Sciences Institute, Las Vegas, Nevada, November 1985.

3. Ernest Alexander, "The Design of Alternatives in Organizational Contexts," *Administrative Science Quarterly* (September 1979): 382–404.

4. Marion B. Folsom, *Executive Decision Making* (New York: McGraw-Hill, 1982), 210.

5. Henry Mintzberg, Duru Raisinghani, and Andre Theoret, "The Structure of Unstructured Decision Processes," *Administrative Science Quarterly* (June 1976): 246–75; Paul Nutt, "Types of Organizational Decision Processes," *Administrative Science Quarterly* (September 1984): 414–50.

6. R. Richard Ritti and G. Ray Funkhouser, *The Ropes to Skip and the Ropes to Know: Studies in Organizational Behavior* (Columbus, Ohio: Grid Publishing, 1979).

7. Chong-Do Hah and Robert Linquist, "The 1952 Steel Seizure Revisited: A Systematic Study of Presidential Decision Making," *Administrative Science Quarterly* (December 1975): 587–605.

8. Arthur VanGundy, *Managing Group Creativity* (New York: AMACOM, 1984), 188–96.

9. Richard O. Mason and Ian I. Mitroff, *Challenging Strategic Planning Assumptions: Theory, Cases, and Techniques* (New York: Wiley, 1981).

10. Ralph H. Kilmann, *Beyond the Quick Fix* (San Francisco: Jossey-Bass, 1984), 141.

11. M. F. Woods and G. B. Davies, "Potential Problem Analysis: A Systematic Approach to Problem Predictions and Contingency Planning—An Aid to the Smooth Exploitation of Research," *R&D Management* 4 (1973): 25–32.

12. Eugene Bardach, *The Implementation Game: What Happens After a Bill Becomes a Law* (Cambridge, Massachusetts: MIT Press, 1977).

13. Randall B. Ripley and Grace A. Franklin, *Bureaucracy and Policy Implementation* (Homewood, Illinois: Dorsey Press, 1982), 21.

14. Peter G. W. Keen and Michael Scott Morton, *Decision Support Systems: An Organizational Perspective* (Reading, Massachusetts: Addison Wesley, 1978).

15. Michael J. Ginzberg, "Early Diagnosis and MIS Implementation Failures: Promising Results and Unanswered Questions," *Management Science* (April 1981): 459–77.

16. Steven Alter, *Decision Support Systems: Current Practice and Continuing Challenges* (Reading, Massachusetts: Addison Wesley, 1980).

17. Ripley and Franklin, *Bureaucracy and Policy Implementation*, 201.

18. VanGundy, *Managing Group Creativity*, 228–29.

19. Bardach, *Implementation Game*, 250–67.

20. Michael J. Ginzberg, "Steps Towards More Effective Implementation Success of MS and MIS," *Interfaces* 8, no. 3 (May 1978): 57–63.

SEVEN

KEYS
to
IMPROVING
TEAM
EFFECTIVENESS

In the previous chapters you learned techniques to improve your problem-solving effectiveness. But improving team effectiveness requires not only individual learning but team learning. And team learning will not take place unless there are departmental or organizational norms that foster creativity, trust, and interteam cooperation. When these are in place you can then design programs to effectively train your staff in the new problem-solving techniques.

BARRIERS TO EFFECTIVE TEAM PERFORMANCE

People who are taught effective problem-solving tools will not automatically be more effective. External factors such as a firm's corporate culture and reward system influence individual and team performance. Bureaucratic values can stifle the most creative problem-solving groups. A reward system that is punitive or that focuses on the individual rather than the team can impede team performance.

Even if the proper norms and reward system are in place, team members may not use the tools they have learned because not all training programs are equally effective. One type of training may not suit everyone; there are individual differences. Unless your training program reflects these differences, meaningful learning may not take place. Even when your staff learns new techniques, there is no guarantee that they will use them. New tools require that we change the way we solve problems. Change is often a difficult process, however, because we are often guided by our emotions rather than by our intellect. Based on follow-up interviews with former workshop participants, here is a sampler of reasons why they do not use the techniques they have "learned":

• I'm still not sure that I know the technique well enough to use it on the job. I understood when the instructor explained it, but now I'm not sure if I can use it.

• I would use the techniques, but my boss won't. So why do it?

• The techniques may work, but they really won't make any difference in my performance evaluation.

• If I only had time to practice what I learned, but I'm so busy.

• I won't get any support in my department because my colleagues have not learned the techniques yet.

What keeps your team from using the new problem-solving techniques on the job? Until you know, you cannot take corrective action. I recommend administering VanGundy's Team Effectiveness Questionnaire on a periodic basis (see Chapter 2, pages 24–26).[1]

This questionnaire is more than an index of team performance. It can help you diagnose the causes of poor team performance. Is it due to cultural, team, or individual factors? You can tell by looking at the subcategory scores. Subcategory scores below 4 are a potential cause of poor team performance. One critical subcategory is the external environment.

External Environmental Factors

External factors include the business your firm is in, its customers and suppliers, and its competition. Some external factors, however, are controllable. The most important are your departmental or company culture and interteam cooperation and communication.

The Cultural Factor

Culture is a pattern of beliefs and expectations shared by organizational members. These beliefs produce norms that powerfully shape the behavior of individuals within organizations.[2] Culture reflects an organization's mission, setting, and what it takes to compete in the marketplace. More important, the founder of the firm and charismatic senior managers imprint their own values onto the corporate culture. Perhaps Lee Iacocca's success at Chrysler is as much due to his "we can do it" value system as it is to his managerial skills.

Senior management's beliefs stem, in part, from individual value systems. The most critical period of value formation is from birth to the early teens. After age 20 or so, few individuals change their values in a dramatic way unless they are jolted by an intense emotional event.

Psychologist Morris Massey classifies individuals into one of the following four values categories:[3]

Traditionalists. These people grew up in the 1920s to the early 1940s. Traditionalists were programmed "like father, like son." They hold rigid expectations about others and believe in a social order with everyone in his or her place. They do not "do their own thing" or "tell it like it is." They are joiners. They love committees, task forces, and organizations that stress teamwork. They believe there is a correct way to do things and readily accept authority figures. Traditionalists bear strong allegiance to their company. They are "tried and true."

In-betweeners. They grew up in the late 1940s and early 1950s. They have been value-programmed by Traditionalists but have also experienced and accepted many new value concepts. They accept the importance of the team approach (Traditionalist) but also believe in individual rights within the organization. They recognize authority but seek participation in the decision-making process. In-betweeners swing between formality and informality and conformity and nonconformity in all aspects of their lives.

Challengers. They grew up in the late 1950s through the early 1970s. They were taught to be less dependent on parents and encouraged to insist on their individual rights. Challengers expect and demand participation. They helped create flextime, day care, and individualized benefit packages. They are concerned with restructuring and revamping institutions. Challengers want to feel good about what they are doing. They accept change and experimentation as a normal part of their lives. Challengers have been taught to question and explore.

Synthesizers. They grew up since the early 1970s and have been exposed to the conflicting values of the three other major generation groups. Their conservative outlook is based on the fact that they see the good life declining. Synthesizers recognize that contemporary problems are difficult. But they reject the simplistic solutions of the Traditionalist (the system will solve the problem) and the Challenger (the system is the problem).

Values transcend one's chronological age. They also depend on the subgroups—social class, ethnic culture, religious background, and so forth—you belong to.

A corporate culture, or set of norms, evolves as the value systems of organizational citizens intermingle. Depending on the corporate culture, norms can range from:

Don't rock the boat.	to	Dare to be different.
Hold your tongue and button your lip.	to	I can disagree with my boss.
Share information with others only if you win.	to	Share information with others.
Look busy even when you are not.	to	Be busy.
Treat women or staff as second-class citizens.	to	All individuals are competent and industrious.
New ideas are bad ideas.	to	New ideas are welcome.

If your division's corporate culture is keeping your team from being effective, you must change it. While value systems are permanent, corporate cultures can be changed.

The Interteam Factor

Team success often depends on the ability to work with other teams or departments. No team is an island unto itself. It may need information or resources from other groups to do its job properly. But often the following problems emerge between members of different teams:[4]

• They avoid one another.
• Needed information or services are not requested.
• Feelings of resentment or hostility occur when the teams interact.
• People feel frustrated or misunderstood by members of other teams with whom they must work.
• Joint projects with other teams are delayed or unsuccessful.

After you have improved the performance of your own team, it is time to seek ways to improve interteam cooperation. Next we will turn to changing departmental culture and improving interteam cooperation and communication.

IMPROVING THE EXTERNAL ENVIRONMENT

Changing Norms

Can your team achieve its mission and goals given its norms? If not, you must change them. Remember that norms evolve from basic values, critical incidents in the team's life, early group behaviors, and carryover behaviors from other organizations or teams. Unlike enduring values, norms can be changed.

How can you extricate yourself from a cultural rut? Using the Nominal Group Technique, ask team members to list the norms that guide their behavior and decision making on the job. Start with a few illustrations to provide guidance. Have team members include norms that deal with task, creativity, social interaction, and personal freedom issues. Have a single spokesperson read all the norms during the round-robin session.

This will assure anonymity and an airing of the true norms. Do not be surprised if many of the norms are negatively stated; for example, "avoid disagreeing with one's boss." Now have the team reach consensus on the most important departmental norms.

Then, using the Nominal Group Technique, ask each person to imagine an ideal team that could accomplish the department or division mission statement. What kind of norms should that team possess? Again focus on task, creativity, social interaction, and personal freedom issues. If the norms "that are" differ from those "that must be," hire an organization development specialist to emend and implement the "must be" norms.

Diagnosing and Minimizing Interteam Problems

Even though you have improved your team's performance, the team may still not perform as effectively as you might wish it would. Often we are hampered by the lack of cooperation with other teams or departments. Diagnosing and minimizing interteam problems is then in order. Begin by identifying which teams should be involved in an interteam team-building meeting. Then ask participants to prepare the following inputs for the initial meeting: (1) their "gut image" of their own team and their perception of other teams, and (2) a statement of their own team culture and their perception of the other teams' cultures.[5]

Have the teams meet in a plenary session and share this information with each other. All teams will gain insight into how others perceive them. For example, team A sees itself as an outstanding corporate citizen. But team B thinks that team A team members are empire builders and power grabbers. Team A believes its members are hard workers, while team B believes that team A only works hard when the task is interesting or self-serving. The joint meeting serves to identify potential sources of conflict among the teams. An organization development specialist should be present to assist with the meeting.

Now have the teams adjourn and meet individually. Have each team reflect on the new data they received from the other teams. Is there any truth to the perception of the other teams?

Teams must be willing to defend their individual cultures but also should be open to new information. Have each team prepare a response to the new insights its members have received.

Now have the groups meet in a second plenary session. In this session the first goal is to reach consensus on the causes of the problems among the teams. Data from the initial session will help diagnose these causes.

Then form subgroups to develop strategies to overcome the causes of interteam conflict and distrust. Place members from several teams on each subgroup. Allow the subgroups to work independently. After the subgroups have formulated their plans, convene a final plenary session. Have each subgroup report its findings. Use the Nominal Group Technique and jointly arrive at a set of action plans. Put the plans into action and monitor progress. It may be necessary to meet on a periodic basis to resolve any further interteam problems.

FACILITATING TRAINING IN PROBLEM-SOLVING METHODS

Skills development in problem finding, diagnosis, alternative generation, and choice is best achieved in formalized training sessions. Reading a book is not sufficient for acquiring these skills. You need to develop in-house workshops for your staff. However, training will be ineffective unless the corporate culture and reward system support it. A performance system that fails to reward effective use of new problem-solving skills will undermine your training. A corporate culture that stifles new ideas will also undermine your training efforts. These external factors must be established prior to initiating team training. Even then, training effectiveness is not assured unless the following administrative and pedagogical factors are in place.

Creating a Need for Training

Unlike accounting or finance, problem solving is not a well-defined body of knowledge. It draws from mathematics, logic, creativity, and the behavioral sciences. Moreover, few managers have ever had a formal course in problem solving. Therefore, they may not even know what problem solving is or that they need training in this area. To be successful you must create a need for training.

Begin by asking your staff members to identify problems they have encountered on the job when making decisions. This will surface areas that need attention in your training program. Using the Nominal Group Technique, cluster these problems into skills development areas. You should augment the list by using my three-stage problem-solving model (Chapter 3). Unlike compulsory education, effective training cannot occur unless participants demand it.

Organizing the Training

Training is most effective when participants are involved in developing the learning objectives and curriculum.[6] After all, participants have significant business experiences that they bring to the training sessions. Treat participants with respect and allow them to help organize the training sessions through the use of planning councils.

Outside consultants or human resource development specialists should help with the program's administration and curriculum. Specialists must walk a tightrope between dictating the program and acquiescing to the demands of the participants. As dictators they run the risk of alienating the participants. As short-order cooks, facilitators can abdicate their responsibility by providing the training that participants want rather than the training they need.

Doing the Training

A department will include personnel with many, if not all, of the eight decision-making styles. Each style learns in different ways. It is important to teach in ways that the trainees will learn best. When this happens, trainees will learn meaningfully and be able to use the problem-solving techniques on the job. Mastery demands that we recognize learning-style differences in teaching problem-solving workshops.[7]

Extroverted Thinker (ET) and Introverted Sensor (IS) are

the two most common decision-making styles (see Exhibit 4-5). ET and IS managers learn quite differently.

Teaching the Extroverted Thinker. Optimal learning occurs when ET trainees work in small groups with others on real problems. The ETs prefer role playing and the use of realistic simulations. They prefer some initial information on the problem-solving tools but learn best when working within small groups where they can learn from one another. Trainers must develop an orderly and logical presentation of materials. ET trainees will also want to know the benefits of the skills they are learning. No benefits, no interest.

Teaching the Introverted Sensor. Optimal learning occurs when IS trainees work individually and have time to reflect on what they are learning. They prefer to work alone on concrete problems and are not interested in the theory underlying the technique. ISs prefer not to work in groups and when required to do so will often be noncommunicative. Unlike their ET counterparts, they prefer lectures to small group exercises.

It will be necessary to tailor your training program to the learning styles of your participants. Remember, they may not learn the way you learn best. Teach the material from their perspective. Include methods that work well for all the decision-making styles.

Evaluating the Training

Unevaluated training is worthless. Your evaluation mechanism must address two issues: Have the sessions achieved their goals? And where do we go from here?

Evaluation must go beyond "feel good" questionnaires administered at the end of the training. Reaction surveys are merely the first of a four-step evaluative process.[8] The next level of evaluation asks: Has learning taken place? Do trainees demonstrate their acquisition of skills? The third level focuses on transference of skills. Are the skills used in work? You should incorporate this level into the annual performance evaluation. Ask your subordinates to document how they have used their newly acquired skills. The fourth level addresses results. Do the new problem-solving skills increase productivity? Productivity and resultant dollar savings are the ultimate test of problem-solving skills acquisition.

After initial training, participants should develop a personal action plan. Adults are inner-directed and desire to continue the learning process on their own.[9] But they need help in formulating personal self-growth programs. These could include additional formal training, books, videotapes, or tutorials. Whatever form the additional learning takes, each trainee should develop a personal action plan after the initial workshops.

Even though your team has been trained in effective problem-solving techniques, it will need refresher sessions. How do you know if your team is not functioning effectively? Look for the following early warning signals of ineffective performance:

• Failure to develop a complete statement of goals or definition of the problem.
• Use of timid search strategies for alternatives.
• Failure to reconsider rejected alternatives.
• Lack of critical thinking.
• Failure to examine the risks associated with their first choice.
• Failure to develop a contingency plan.
• Domination and direction of the discussion by a senior person.

Rather than waiting for problems, monitor your group's behavior on a periodic basis. Set aside time for metadecision making. Examine how you reach decisions and solve problems. What did the team do correctly? How can it improve? Use the Team Process Critique Questionnaire from Chapter 3. Have each member complete it anonymously and return it to you. Now the team is ready to improve its own processes. Alternatively, consider videotaping an actual problem-solving session. Using the Nominal Group Technique, critique the meeting and identify areas in need of further improvement. Or schedule a team meeting and use the Nominal Group Technique to develop a set of action plans to improve team processes. If more formal training is needed, ask a human resources development facilitator to help you develop a new curriculum for your refresher training.

A FINAL THOUGHT

We end the book—as we began it—with a challenge. You have already solved the NASA Moon Survival Test. Now here's the rest of the story.

On board the spaceship was a father and his son. The father was killed and the boy suffered a broken leg in the crash. After locating the ship, a space ambulance took the boy to the hospital at the nearby moon base. The boy was wheeled into the emergency operating room. The surgeon was about to operate. Suddenly the surgeon cried out: "I can't operate on this boy. He's my son!"

Can you explain what's going on?[10]

ENDNOTES

1. Arthur VanGundy, *Managing Group Creativity* (New York: AMACOM, 1984), 54–56.

2. H. Schwartz and S. Davis, "Matching Corporate Culture and Business Strategy," *Organizational Dynamics* (Summer 1981): 30–48.

3. Massey Values Analysis Profile, Morris Massey Performax Systems International, Inc., 1981.

4. W. Dyer, *Team Building: Issues and Alternatives* (Reading, Massachusetts: Addison Wesley, 1977), 118.

5. Ralph Kilmann, *Beyond the Quick Fix* (San Francisco: Jossey-Bass, 1984), 252–57.

6. Stephen Brookfield, *Understanding and Facilitating Adult Learning* (San Francisco: Jossey-Bass, 1986), 10.

7. Isabel Briggs Myers and Mary McCaulley, *Manual: A Guide to Development and Use of The Myers-Briggs Type Indicator* (Palo Alto, California: Consulting Psychologist Press, 1985), 130–33.

8. D. Kirkpatrick, "Evaluation of Training" in *Training and Development Handbook*, ed. R. Craig and L. Bittel (New York: McGraw-Hill, 1967).

9. M. Knowles and Associates, *Andragogy in Action: Applying Modern Principles of Adult Learning* (San Francisco: Jossey-Bass, 1984).

10. The surgeon was the boy's mother.

ANSWER TO NASA MOON SURVIVAL GAME

Item	Rank	Reason
Box of matches	15	Useless since no oxygen.
Food concentrates	4	Satisfied basic energy requirements.
50 feet of nylon rope	6	Useful in scaling cliffs, tying injured.
Parachute silk	8	Protection from sun's rays.
Portable heating unit	13	Only useful on dark side of the Moon.
Two .45 caliber pistols	11	Possible source of propulsion.
1 case of dehydrated milk	12	Duplicates food concentrates and is bulkier.
200-pound tanks of oxygen	1	Absolute necessity for life support.
Stellar maps (of Moon's constellations)	3	Important means of determining directions.
Life raft	9	CO_2 bottle possible propulsion device.
Magnetic compass	14	Useless since magnetic field is not polarized.
5 gallons of water	2	Absolute necessity to sustain life.
Signal flares	10	Possible distress signal once close enough to mother ship.
First aid kit including injection needles	7	Injection needles fitted to suit apertures useful.
Solar powered FM receiver/transmitter	5	Useful only if line of sight transmission is possible.

GLOSSARY

ALTERNATIVE WORLDVIEW METHOD: A diagnostic method for determining causes in which subgroups begin with different assumptions about causes and seek a synthesis position.

ANALOGY METHOD: A creative method used to generate alternative solutions.

ANCHORING EFFECT: Anchoring occurs when junior members of a group cannot generate ideas that are vastly different from the senior members' initial ideas.

ASSUMPTION-SURFACING METHOD: Subgroups generate and debate critical assumptions underlying alternatives to determine the best solution.

AUXILIARY MODE: The psychological function of sensing, intuition, thinking, or feeling that a manager uses to support his or her dominant mode.

CHARTER: Describes how a team will operate and what is expected from each member.

COHESIVENESS: The degree of mutual attraction that members have for each other and the group.

CONTINGENCY PLAN: An essential ingredient in a difficult implementation; includes what action to take and when to take it if the installation is threatened.

COUNTER-IMPLEMENTOR(S): An individual or group whose goal is to stop the implementation of a solution.

CULTURE: A pattern of beliefs and expectations shared by organizational members. The pattern produces cultural norms that powerfully shape the behavior of individuals within organizations.

DECISION GOALS: The goals you hope to achieve in solving a problem.

DECISION-MAKING STYLE: Refers to how you orient your life and how you acquire and process information. Based on Carl Jung's writings.

DEVIL'S ADVOCATE: A role in a group in which one or more members attempt to find weaknesses with the alternative under consideration.

DIAGNOSIS: Refers to either determining causes of a problem or reformulating the decision goals.

DISCUSSION GROUP: A group structure that encourages anchoring, inequality of participation, and self-censorship.

DISTURBANCE PROBLEM: A deviation from historical or budgeted performance levels. Diagnosis means determining the causes of the deviation.

DOMINANT MODE: The psychological function of sensing, intuition, thinking, or feeling that a manager uses most of the time.

ENTREPRENEURIAL PROBLEM: A deviation between a present performance level and where management envisions that the department should or could be. Diagnosis means reformulating desired decision goals.

5Ws METHOD: A creative method for either reformulating decision goals or identifying potential problems during implementation.

GAMESMANSHIP MODEL: Useful in suggesting tactics that counter-implementors play to delay or stop the installation of an alternative solution.

GANTT CHART: A diagram that shows the sequence of steps and the amount of time required to implement a solution. Useful in managing the installation process.

GOAL REFORMULATION: The key to diagnosing an entrepreneurial problem. A way to consider alternative decision goals.

GROUPTHINK: A consensus-at-any-cost mentality that drains the critical thinking powers of cohesive groups when they are under extreme stress.

HETEROGENEOUS GROUPS: Teams consisting of members from different functional disciplines or decision-making styles.

HEURISTIC: A rule of thumb that helps managers to quickly process information. Can cause managers to draw incorrect inferences or conclusions.

ILL-STRUCTURED PROBLEMS: Complex problems in which there is no agreement on the causes or procedures for solving them.

IMPLEMENTATION: A process that ensures that you successfully install your solution. It involves the unfreezing, moving, and refreezing stages.

INFERIOR MODE: The psychological function of sensing, intuition, thinking, or feeling that a manager uses least often.

INFORMATION-SHARING TEAMS: The team generates and is involved in diagnosis and alternative generation, but the leader makes the final decision.

MATRIX-WEIGHTING METHOD: A method for selecting the best alternative when there are many alternatives generated. You rank order the decision goals and determine the degree to which each alternative accomplishes each goal.

METADECISION MAKING: A process of auditing and thereby improving your team's decision-making processes.

MORAL ALGEBRA METHOD: Developed by Benjamin Franklin, moral algebra is a systematic method for screening a large number of alternatives prior to choice making.

MOVING STAGE: The second of Lewin and Schein's three stages of implementation. Here you install the solution.

NOMINAL GROUP TECHNIQUE: A group structure that ensures that all members participate in the deliberations. Developed by Van de Ven and Delbecq.

NORMS: Rules and procedures that teams develop to organize and control their behaviors.

PARTICIPATIVE PROBLEM SOLVING: Occurs when the team is involved in diagnosis and alternative generation and results in a final decision.

PERFECT PROBLEM SOLVER: A manager who uses the four psychological functions of sensing, intuition, thinking, and feeling equally well. Perfect problem solvers do not exist.

POTENTIAL PROBLEM ANALYSIS: Helps is to determine what could go wrong during an installation.

PREFORMAL CLOSURE: The tendency to reject alternative solutions before formally evaluating them.

PROBLEM-FINDING TEAMS: Teams whose goal is to identify latent problems or emerging opportunities within a department.

RATIONAL ARGUMENTATION MODEL: Helps managers present the reasoning behind their claims.

REFREEZING STAGE: The last of Lewin and Schein's three stages of implementation. Here you turn over the solution to the problem havers, and the solution becomes an accepted part of the organization.

RINGII: A decision-making procedure developed by the Japanese in which a written document is sent from member to member and edited by each member without any person-to-person interaction.

SCENARIO WRITING: A strategy for developing a contingency plan when political infighting can be expected during installation. Team members determine how counter-implementors will delay an installation and then develop tactics to beat them.

SECOND-LOOK MEETING: Serves two purposes—first, you reconsider options that were rejected during screening or choice; second, you seek to uncover potential problems that might arise during implementation.

SKELETAL IDEA: An executive summary or overview that can be written on a single page. It should include a brief description of an idea with its rationale and very rough estimates of the costs and benefits.

STAKEHOLDERS: Individuals or groups who affect or are affected by a solution. Managers often implicitly and incorrectly assume what various stakeholders want, believe, expect, or value.

STATUS: A person's rank within a firm; is legitimated by the trappings of one's office—status symbols.

UNFREEZING STAGE: The first of Lewin and Schein's three stages of implementation. Here you create the need for problem solving by finding problems or opportunities.

VALUES: Fundamental beliefs that provide meaning for and drive our lives.

VENTURE GROUP: A team whose job is to find latent problems or emerging opportunities.

INDEX